DEFENDERS OF THE REICH

Jagdgeschwader 1

Volume Three

1944-1945

Other titles in this work

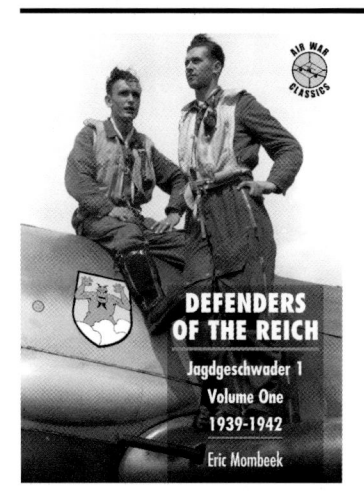

DEFENDERS OF THE REICH
Jagdgeschwader 1
Volume One
1939-1942
Eric Mombeek

DEFENDERS OF THE REICH
Jagdgeschwader 1
Volume Two
1943
Eric Mombeek

CLASSIC
An imprint of
Ian Allan Publishing

First published 2003

ISBN 1 903223 03 2

All rights reserved. No part of this book may be reproduced or transmitted in any form or by any means, electronic or mechanical including photocopying or by any information storage and retrieval system without permission from the Publisher in writing.

© Robert Forsyth, Eddie Creek and Eric Mombeek 2003
© Colour Artwork: Thomas Tullis 2003

Produced by Chevron Publishing Limited
Project Editor: Robert Forsyth
Cover and book design by Colin Woodman Design

Published by Classic Publications

an imprint of Ian Allan Publishing Ltd, Hersham, Surrey KT12 4RG, England
Printed by Ian Allan Printing Ltd, Hersham, Surrey KT12 4RG, England

Visit the Classic Publications website at www.classic-books.co.uk

JG 1

DEFENDERS OF THE REICH

Jagdgeschwader 1

Volume Three

1944-1945

Eric Mombeek

Acknowledgements

Compiled over some ten years, the realisation of this work would not have been possible without the help of many people who were good enough to meet me or to allow me to enter into lengthy correspondence. Furthermore, many researchers willingly and generously opened their archives for me and offered me their help.

A number of former members of JG 1 or their families (F) gave me their valuable cooperation:
Mrs and MM. Alvensleben von A., Augner K., Berger H., Bekker K., Biederbick H., Braune E., Brustellin H-H (F), Buchholz G. (F), Buchholz E. (F), Burath E., Burckhardt L.-W. (F), Clade E., Demuth E., Dietrich W., Dobislav M. (F), Dosch H., Dürr A., Düsterbeck J., Eberle F.(F), Eder G. (F), Eh H., Ell K., Enderle F. (F), Engleder R., Ernst W., Ertmann H. (F), Falck W., Framm G.(F), Franzisket L. (F), Freudendorfer A., Friedrich E., Gerold L., Gräfe W. (F), Grislawski A., Gutowski W., Halbey H., Hanf G., Harder W., Haspel F., Hausotter H., Heckmann G., Heesen E. (F), Hennig O., Hildenbrand G., Hillmer D., Hoepfner W., Hofmann F., Hollmann, Hübl R., Ibing K., Ihlefeld H., Janke J., Job A., Kageneck v. E. (F), Kaiser H., Kehrle J., Kinsky F.(F), Kirchmayr von R., Klöpper H. (F), Köditz W., Köhne W., Kortzfleisch v. B., Krell G., Kremer K., Kretschmer W., Künneke H., Lacha M. (F), Leesmann K.-H. (F), Lehmann H-G., Lindenschmidt A.(F), Losigkeit F., Luckenbach S., Maul H., Meissner H., Michalski A., Miksch A.(F), Mix E.(F), Moldenhauer H., Moritz W., Neuner H., Pirkenseer F., Pretsch v. Lerchenhorst H., Rahner E., Rauhaus R. (F), Rauth T. (F), Rettich H., Reinhardt H-G., Rudschinat S., Sannemann H., Schiele O., Schmid O., Schnappauf R. (F), Schuhmacher L., Selbach H. (F), Selle v.E.(F), Siegfried L., Snaidero F., Sperling H-J., Staerk E. (F), Steeb E., Steiner F., Sundermeier K-H., Timpe F., Wedding W.-K., Wedel E., Wegner F., Wennekers H-G., Wickop D. (F), Widmann W., Wintergerst E.(F), Wollenweber W., Zander F. (F).

Bob Milliken also kindly assisted with his recollections.

The following enthusiasts also gave their kind assistance:
Barbas B., Bowman M., Caldwell D., Campion D., Chuinard R., Crow J., Decobeck R., De Decker C., de Visser R.W., Hiller A., Kitchens J., Lorant J-Y., Maesel K., Manrho J., Meyer M., Mol K., Neeven A, Oeltjebrunns W., Petrick P., Ring H., Roba J-L, Sommerau-Fernandez M., Stewart A., Taghon P., Vanhee C., Van Mol J-P, Vasco J., Watteeuw P., White R., Zimmermann F.

My thanks also to Eddie Creek and Robert Forsyth at Chevron Publishing.

To all of them, my sincerest gratitude.

Sources

Most *Luftwaffe* archives were destroyed during the last weeks of the Second World War. Only one war diary of JG 1 remains, namely, that of II./JG 1. Held in the Bundesarchiv-Militärarchiv in Freiburg, this document (though it ends with of the Normandy Invasion of 6 June 1944), was of invaluable importance and later, following the publication of the first version of this study, the author was able to use microfilms containing a significant part of the JG 1 claims. The relatively complete loss tables (only 1944 is missing), are to be found in the WASt. in Berlin. These documents formed the basis of my research. But the history of JG 1 would not have been possible to tell without the help of former members of JG 1 (or their families) who contributed personal notes, memories and last but not least, several log books detailing numerous missions.

Author's Note

An appendix to this work, detailing the claims of enemy aircraft damaged or destroyed by *Jagdgeschwader* 1 between 1939-1945 and a table of losses can be found on the *Jagdgeschwader* 1 page of the author's website at http://membres.lycos.fr/mombeek/

CONTENTS

"To do our duty, even unto death..."
1944 – Year of Decision …… 206

Berlin Debut …… 225

"Indescribable chaos..."
The Invasion Front – June-July 1944 …… 246

"Enemy fighters were always lying in wait..."
Retreat – August 1944 …… 259

"Achtung! Indianer behind us!"
Return to the Reich …… 264

'Bodenplatte' …… 280

JG 1 in the East …… 284

The Peoples' Fighter
February-April 1945 …… 291

The End
April-May 1945 …… 296

Chapter Sixteen

"To do our duty, even unto death..."
1944 – Year of Decision

The year 1943 marked a decisive turning point for the Third Reich. It was also a significant time for *Jagdgeschwader* 1 and for German fighter aviation as a whole. On the threshold of the New Year, the *Wehrmacht* found itself retreating on all fronts. Russia, assisted by the industrial might of the United States, had succeeded in building up a formidable army equipped with seemingly limitless resources. German forces, on the other hand, could only attempt to hold up Soviet efforts at reconquering lost territory which, at this time, were concentrated in the area around Kiev. In the Mediterranean, the Germans held, at great cost, the centre of the southern Italian front, thus preventing Allied forces streaming north. To the west, preparations were being made to repel the inevitable Allied invasion, which would, almost certainly, determine the outcome of the war.

In the air, German fighters continued to record significant results. In the east, the figures spoke for themselves; on 14 October 1943, Walter Nowotny, *Kommandeur* of I./JG 54, became the first pilot to reach 250 victories. Less than two months later, JG 52 celebrated its 8,000th victory. Nevertheless, German losses increased and the *Luftwaffe* was no longer master of the skies. In the west, the *Jagdwaffe* had been seriously depleted due to high rates of combat attrition. However, the progressive reinforcement of Reich defence units allowed them to continue to achieve satisfactory results during the ever-increasing daylight raids.

But the future for the 1,650 German fighters assembled in the West did not bode well. By the end of December 1943, ten more *Ritterkreuzträger* had been lost, one each from JG 1, JG 11 and JG 27 respectively, two each from JG 2 and JG 26 and three from JG 3. The Allies were working to extend the range of their escort fighters. On 13 December, P-47s were able to reach Kiel. By March 1944, P-47s, P-38s and P-51s accompanied American bombers as far as Berlin. This formidable and effective Allied escort altered the balance of power between the opposing forces and the opening of 1944 marked the turning point. Though JG 2 *Richthofen*, based in the Brittany-Normandy region, and JG 26 in northern France and Belgium, celebrated 2,000 victories on 15 January and 24 February 1944 respectively, their ebullience soon dissipated as all realistic hope of resisting the colossal superiority of Allied air power progressively disappeared.

Oblt. Eberhard Burath recalled those days: "From the beginning of 1944, the war became extremely hard for us. The time had long since gone when we entered combat 'fresh and happy'. It wasn't exactly a feeling of fear, but rather a state of excitement, of extreme tension. Calmness and joking had totally disappeared, yet, in spite of that, there remained a firm resolution to overcome fear and to do our duty, even unto death. In flying, when the enemy were found, and combat could no longer be avoided, all sentiment disappeared. You became a war machine. You became all-powerful. Shortly after landing, you were worn out by the change. One tried to forget things by drinking. We sometimes did not know how we could carry on ...

"We did not sleep a lot; we would drink and talk for a great part of the night. On early morning scrambles, I often took off with my flying gear rapidly thrown over my pyjamas. A good whiff of oxygen quickly woke me up. Our way of life was very special, and that is why we stayed, in the main, on our airfield. Even during times of respite, there was a certain tension; an alert could surprise us at any moment. In such cases, the contrast was enormous; we would leave our chairs to enter into murderous combat several minutes later. Less than two hours later, we would once again be stretched out in the sun. It was even harder to take when a friend's chair remained empty."

Lt. Hans Berger recalled his early days with the unit: "When I arrived at I./JG 1, on 12 June 1943, I was a very fearless pilot, and ten days later I shot down my first B-17. I saw several crew members bale out, and I followed the aircraft down until it crashed. I was therefore able to pinpoint its location precisely. The remains were exactly where I had indicated. However, without a witness, this victory was not credited to me. Being a young, inexperienced officer, I had little chance of having it confirmed. My first 'kill' simply allowed a more experienced pilot to move a little nearer to receiving the *Ritterkreuz*. My first disappointment. The second was much worse. I had a very good friend, my *Schwarmführer*, Johannes Rathenow. He taught me a lot and I appreciated his kindness. On 3 November 1943, while manoeuvring into position to attack a box of *Viermots*, his aircraft received a direct hit and exploded before my eyes. I was only a few metres to his left.

Obstlt. Walter 'Gulle' Oesau, a top pilot with more than 100 'kills', succeeded Obstlt. Hans Philipp as Kommodore of JG 1 in late 1943. He is seen here upon his arrival with the unit.

"These two events, and the circumstances of the situation in which we fought, completely changed my view of the war. Those who chased the honours list would very quickly find their name on a loss list. My comrades laughed at me when they saw me underlining the different aerodromes on a map. I systematically remembered all the small landing grounds where I might eventually gain refuge after pursuing a stream of bombers. We were often short of fuel and had to get down quickly. Frequently all these places were under surveillance from enemy fighters who pounced on us as soon as our undercarriage came down. I, myself, contrived to remain alone and avoid these 'hot' areas. Landing on a small base offered the following advantages; firstly, fighter pilots were always particularly well received there and were well fed; secondly, you did not have to take off immediately with unfamiliar pilots who disappeared, leaving you to face the enemy alone and, thirdly, these small airfields often did not possess the special 'C' fuel required by fighter aircraft. I could therefore expect a respite of two or three days. It was perhaps because of these factors that I survived."

Following the New Year revelry (I. *Gruppe* had been provided with 5,000 litres of beer!), it was difficult to get back to the serious business of fighting a war. At the start of the year the composition of the *Jagdgeschwader* was as follows:

Stab JG 1 at Deelen
under *Obstlt*. Walter Oesau
Fw 190 A – 4 (1)
I./JG 1 at Dortmund
under *Major* Emil-Rudolf Schnoor
Fw 190 A – 29 (27)
II./JG 1 at Rheine
under *Hptm*. Walter Hoeckner
Fw 190 A – 21 (17)
III./JG 1 at Volkel
under *Hptm*. Friedrich Eberle
Bf 109 G – 42 (36)

At the end of 1943, a respected and highly accomplished officer joined the unit from the fighter training school at Orange in France. Known for his straight talking throughout the *Luftwaffe*, the arrival of *Major* Heinz Bär was welcomed by II. *Gruppe*. Göring had not showered many honours on him, in spite of his being credited with 178 victories on all fronts and in spite of previously serving as *Staffelkapitän* and *Gruppen-kommandeur* in several units. With JG 1 however, Bär was a simple *Staffelführer*, initially assigned to lead 11. *Staffel*, which, ironically, was about to be dissolved. As a result, he was transferred quickly to 6./JG 1. His relatively low-standing in the unit was supposed to be seen as a form of disgrace following several bluntly-expressed opinions which did not concur with the *Reichsmarschall's* personal, but largely unrealistic perception of air strategy. Several renowned pilots gravitated to this *Staffel*. Following the accidental death of *Oblt*. Harry Koch, *Oblt*. Lutz-Wilhelm Burckhardt, a *Ritterkreuzträger* with over 50 victories in the east and who previously commanded I./JG 77 in Italy, took command of the *Staffel*. Just like Bär, he had fallen into disgrace at his former unit and as a kind of 'punishment' was sent to the Reich (a third pilot from JG 77, and another *Ritterkreuzträger*, Herbert Kaiser would soon follow the same way and join JG 1 and it is worthy of note that all these pilots survived the war). However, Burckhardt, having always flown the Bf 109, he moved to III. *Gruppe* on 9 February 1944 to become *Staffelkapitän* of 7. *Staffel*. This *Staffel* had been depleted in strength by recent operations; in two and a half months three *Staffelkapitäne* had been lost. *Oblt*. Georg 'Schorsch' Eder took over 6. *Staffel*. He left hospital after being wounded on 5 November 1943 whilst with JG 2, whose 5. *Staffel* he had led. He had more than 30 victories when he joined JG 1. In spite of their ability, these pilots acknowledged the prowess of Bär. It was he who led II. *Gruppe* from the time he joined it. Moreover, the *Gruppenkommandeur*, *Hptm*. Walter Hoeckner, was in the throes of being transferred to I./JG 4 in Italy, and his successor, *Hptm*. Hermann Segatz, from JG 5, was clever enough to understand Bär's uncommon aptitudes. The pilots were unanimous: Bär was the natural choice to lead the *Gruppe*.

The year 1944 opened with a bad start for I./JG 1. On 4 January, the *Gruppe* encountered American fighters in the Münster area. Two pilots were killed without any claims. Similarly, III./JG 1 lost *Fhj-Fw*. Albert Lindenschmid, an experienced pilot. *Fw*. Heinz Fuchs of 6./JG 1, flying Fw 190 A-6 'White 2', was the only pilot accredited with shooting down a B-17 that day.

He wrote of the action: "On 4 January 1944, I scrambled with the *Gruppe* at 10.05 hrs as a *Rottenführer* (leader of a two aircraft element) of 4./JG 1. At 10.20 hrs, as we were at 4,000 metres height, we saw at 7,000 metres south-west of Münster, two 'boxes' of around 40 Flying Fortresses, each with a good fighter escort. I climbed to a Boeing some 500 metres behind the others. Despite the fact that Thunderbolts were hanging 100 metres over it, I made two attacks from the rear flying as near as possible. One of its starboard engines was destroyed and a part of the fuselage and the fin exploded. The Boeing lost a lot

Major Heinz Bär arrived at Rheine in early January 1944. Despite his experience and his numerous victories, he was relegated to 6./JG 1 as a 'humble' pilot by Reichsmarschall Göring who did not appreciate his blunt 'talk'. Within five months, Bär would command successively the Staffel, the Gruppe and finally the Geschwader. With a victory tally standing at 221, Bär died in a sports aircraft crash on 28 April 1957.

LEFT AND ABOVE: Hptm. Friedrich Eberle photographed with his Bf 109 'White 20'. Appointed Gruppenkommandeur of III./JG 1 on 9 October 1943, he held this position until 27 April 1944. In the summer of 1944, he took command of III./JG 4 and survived the war.

RIGHT: Geschwaderkommodore, Obstlt. Walter Oesau returns from a mission.

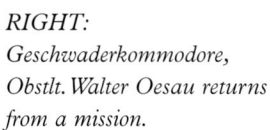

BELOW: In early February 1944, Hptm. Hoeckner, seen here on the left in conversation with his Kommodore, Obstlt. Oesau, left II./JG 1 in order to take command of I./JG 4.

ABOVE: Obstlt. Walter Oesau, Kommodore of JG 1, chats with members of Stab II./JG 1 at Rheine, early 1944. From left: Hptm. Ernst Staerk (Gruppenadjutant), Hptm. Walter Hoeckner (Gruppenkommandeur), the Kommodore and an unknown officer.

of height. As I launched my third attack (from the side), I myself became the target for the Thunderbolts. My aircraft was nearly ripped apart, and was hit so many times on the wings and the fin that I had to break my attack and try to land as soon as possible. My *Rottenflieger* (wingman), *Ofw.* Liper, saw the B-17 I had attacked for the last time at 2,000 metres. It crashed at 12.00 hrs in square JN 5/5 (Zeddam – 10 km N. of Emmerich)."

Fuchs's Fw 190 A-6 'White 2' (W.Nr. 470077) had fired 300 rounds with its MG 17 and 368 more with its MG 151/20. One American crewman from the B-17 was killed and another was captured. The eight survivors may have been helped to escape by the Dutch resistance.

Losses for 5 January were also very high. The *Geschwaderstab* claimed two B-24s (one each for the *Kommodore*, *Obstlt.* Oseau, and his wingman, *Hptm.* Maier-ten-Doornkaat), but I. *Gruppe* paid a heavy price for its sole victory (*Lt.* Ehlers) and four B-17 *Herausschüsse*; three pilots killed, including the very experienced *Fw.* Bernhard Kunze of 2. *Staffel*.

On 11 January, II./JG 1 enjoyed its first major success of the year. The American 1st, 2nd and 3rd Bomb Divisions sent nearly 600 aircraft to bomb aircraft production centres at Oschersleben and Halberstadt, as well as other targets in central Germany. At around 10.30 hrs, all three *Gruppen* of the unit were scrambled. I. *Gruppe* was the first to meet the bombers and the unit immediately claimed three victories, one of them, the 120th for *Hptm.* Alfred Grislawski. Fifteen pilots from II./JG 1 hit 60 B-17s over Paderborn. Three successive head-on attacks by the *Gruppe* led by *Oblt.* von Kirchmayr resulted in the impressive result of nine B-17s claimed as shot down, although only two pilots were officially credited (Rüdiger von Kirchmayr flying Fw 190 A-7 'Black 1' [W.Nr. 430172], and Leo Schuhmacher). Among the claimants were *Oberleutnante* Burath and von Kirchmayr (2); *Leutnant* Wegner, *Feldwebeln* Fuchs and Kirchner (who claimed two B-17s before being wounded and making an emergency-landing). The *Gruppe* lost *Uffz.* Erwin Mietho, *Oblt.* Koch's former wingman. After quickly refuelling, elements of I. and III./JG 1 took off again shortly before 13.00 hrs. They recorded five more victories and one *Herausschuss* over Zwolle in central Holland including a P-47 and B-17 claimed by *Oblt.* Overhagen and a B-17 claimed by *Lt.* Berger. Sixty American bombers did not return that day and the Americans described the German fighter reaction as "intense".

ABOVE: Pilots of Sturmstaffel 1 and I./JG 1 gather on the rain-damp perimeter road at Dortmund, early 1944. First on the left is Oblt. Wilhelm Krebs and in front of him, Hptm. Alfred Grislawski. To the extreme right is Ofw. Gerhard Vivroux of the Sturmstaffel. Lt. Herbert Eh of 3./JG 1 remembers that volunteers were called to step forward to reinforce the Sturmstaffel. No pilots from I./JG 1 volunteered.

LEFT: Recognisable in this photograph is Hptm. Günther Wrobel (first left), Ofw. Erich Kaiser (third left), Ofw. Emil Demuth (fifth left). Facing the camera (from left to right), Major Hans-Günther von Kornatzki (commander of Sturmstaffel 1), Oberst Walter Grabmann, and with back to camera, Hptm. Alfred Grislawski.

LEFT: On 11 January 1944, II./JG 1 underwent its first major engagement in three weeks. Eleven B-17s were claimed by ten of the unit's fifteen operational pilots that day led by Oblt. Rüdiger von Kirchmayr. Seen after landing (from left to right): Lt. Wegner, Ofw. Schuhmacher, Oblt. von Kirchmayr, Ofw. Hanninger, Oblt. Burath, Fw. Sauer, St.Fw. Martens, and Fw. Schönrock. All of them made claims.

BELOW: Hptm. Alfred Grislawski, Staffelkapitän of 1./JG 1, decribes his latest combat and possibly his victory on 11 January 1944. On the 24th, he was injured following another 'Abschuss' and was forced to bale out of his Fw 190 A-7.

ABOVE: St.Fw. Rudolf Martens of 5./JG 1 about to jump down from his Fw 190 A-6 'Black 9' (W.Nr. 550755) at Rheine, 11 January 1944. He was shot down and killed by P-47s in this aircraft 13 days later.

On 24 January, heavy combat took place in the skies over Belgium. A force of 563 bombers escorted by 678 fighters were sent to the Frankfurt area, but the bad weather disorganised the armada. The bombers were recalled and returned to England. Nevertheless, one group of 60 bombers dropped their bombs on the electric power station near Eschweiler. Twenty-one aircraft of II./JG 1 encountered around 50 bombers. Two of the escorting P-51s and two P-38s were claimed for the loss of three pilots killed and two wounded on the German side. Among those killed were a *Schwarmführer* of 5. *Staffel*, *St.Fw.* Rudolf Martens and his wingman, *Lt.* Harald Schilling, shot down by P-47s in the Tournai area. I. *Gruppe*, led by the *Staffelkapitän* of 1. *Staffel*, *Hptm.* Alfred Grislawski, were also in action, with Grislawski being shot down and baling out wounded after claiming a new victory. The *Gruppe* also claimed three *Herausschüsse* by *Lt.* Hans Berger, *Uffz.* Rudolf Hübl and *Ofw.* Emil Demuth. *Fw.* Martin Saller of 3./JG 1 was killed during the action.

On 30 January, the three *Gruppen* were once again in action and this time they were up against 777 bombers and 635 fighters whose objectives were Braunschweig and Hannover. Twelve victories were claimed in total by JG 1. Several pilots increased their victory tally; *Lt.* Hans Ehlers recorded his 34th and 35th; *Ofw.* Anton Piffer his 19th and 20th; *Major* Emil Schnoor his 15th and *Oberst* Oesau his 107th. Four pilots of II. *Gruppe*, *Fw.* Sauer, *Uffz.* Rauhaus, *Uffz.* Swoboda and *Uffz.* Negressus, each claimed a B-17 thus bringing II. *Gruppe*'s total score to 600 victories. In contrast, III. *Gruppe*, sorely tested, suffered the loss of six pilots killed, among them the *Staffelkapitän* of 7. *Staffel*, *Hptm.* Albert Kind. Three pilots were wounded, including *Gruppenkommandeur*, *Hptm.* Friedrich Eberle.

On 8 February, the three *Gruppen* were in action towards midday against heavies on a mission to bomb marshalling yards in Frankfurt. I. *Gruppe* claimed six B-17s with *Lt.* Hans Berger, *Major* Emil Schnoor, *Ofw.* Anton Piffer and *Fw.* Walter Köhne among the claimants. The *Kommodore*, Walter Oesau claimed a P-38, while a P-47 was shot down by *Uffz.* Herbert Dosch of II. *Gruppe*.

For the pilots, it was impossible to accept the loss of both friends and enemy, despite such loss becoming a daily occurrence. The list of the dead grew longer and longer as the days passed.

"Even the most experienced of us lost our nerve at times," remembered Eberhard Burath. "Before take-off, one risked getting lost in the cigarette smoke. The majority of pilots were withdrawn, unapproachable. Only *Major* Bär did not change. At every stage of 'readiness', we just waited to get off quickly. At 30 minutes readiness, we wandered around the airfield. At 15 minutes, we remained near dispersal and checked our equipment. At three minutes, we put on our flying suits and leather boots, plus life jacket, flask of colourant, pistol and flares if we were operating near the coast; around the waist went the compass; the map, paper with all the codes as well as chocolate and pervitine in the knee pouch. Orders were passed by loudspeaker or by telephone. In the case of a scramble not involving cockpit readiness, we would run to our machines. Between two and four mechanics would help us. One would be on the left wing to help us to get into the aircraft and attach our parachute which was already in place on the seat. The rest of the equipment had been prepared in advance: dinghy, earphones, sunglasses… We tested the radio and checked the oxygen. During this time, two other mechanics helped to start the engine. We then taxied to the take-off point, and then took off in formation. Different coloured flares indicated in which order the different *Staffeln* were to take off.

"On 10 February, it happened once again. It was a memorable day. I flew as wingman to an experienced *Oberfeldwebel*. We met up with a formation of *Viermots* over Braunschweig. My comrade attacked alone and immediately shot down a B-17. *Now you do it* – I told myself – *Go on, after them!* I approached very close to my victim and fired a long burst at him. His right wing was badly hit, and flames spewed out. Nevertheless, the Americans did not give up and continued to fire at me. My aircraft was hit all over. Like lightning flashes, the bullets ripped into the fuselage. Soon, there was no response from the joy-stick, or from the other controls. I did not know what to do to get out! I had already jettisoned the canopy but, like a stamp on an envelope, I remained stuck to the armour plate in the cockpit. My right arm was finally out, but forced by the wind, it was pushed backwards. I forced my head out and to the side. I felt that my nostrils resembled those of a charging stallion. My left hand caught hold of the front of the canopy and I pulled. In this situation, the force was enough, and I was carried clear by an air current. My breathing was blocked, and the wind played with my jacket and tore it. One of my boots was forced off, and I was thrown about like a table-tennis ball. *Don't pull! Don't pull!* Pulling the ripcord just after baling out would be foolish. I was falling very fast, I was too high, and furthermore, the sky was full of enemy aircraft. I had already seen personally how they machine-gunned defenceless pilots hanging on their parachutes. *Faster, faster, lose altitude!*

"Thankfully, things calmed down a bit then. The speed decreased and I pulled myself together. I realised that I was falling head first. My legs were tossing about above me. Above, all remained calm. The top of the clouds spread out for about 2,000 metres. At this height I could open the parachute. A 4,000 metre descent is not too bad! I approached the clouds. No fighters in sight, so I pulled the ripcord and the canopy deployed. I felt the shock as the parachute opened. But everything went fine. I had been 'floating' for several moments when my attention was drawn to a sound. A small black spot fell in front of me – I wanted to put out my hand and catch my boot! In the clouds, my anxiety returned. I could see nothing. *How do I get out of this?* Shortly afterwards, a dull colour came towards me – the earth was in view. My adventure was reaching its end, even if there still was a little more to come. *Where should I land?* On the ground, there were trees everywhere, and I had no desire to pin my backside to one. Up to now, everything had gone well, but this was rather bad … I then felt a small fresh breeze which, without effort, pushed me further on. Roofs… a church… a complete village. This looked no better. I saw people in the street and I cried. Some looked up with fear on their faces. The village disappeared beneath me and a freshly ploughed field came into view. A few seconds later I hit the earth. *At last!* I was sprawled on my

Hopsten: two P-47s have just strafed I./JG 1's airfield. A Ju 88 burns in the background. On the right is Fw 190 A-7 'White 20' of the Gruppenstab.

stomach. There was no way of releasing the parachute, the mud had blocked up the buckle. I was there, on all fours in a field, the silk wrapped all around me. I looked like a pig trying to find a truffle. The ground was covered in snow…"

In the sky above Burath, the battle raged. *Major* Heinz Bär, who was leading II. *Gruppe*, shot down a B-17 and a P-47. The II. *Gruppe's* final reckoning was eight victories and one *Herausschuss* for one German pilot – *Lt.* Rudolf Kaschichke of 4. *Staffel* – killed. I. *Gruppe* was also in action and claimed the destruction of six B-17s with *Fw.* Rudolf Hübl, *Ofw.* Emil Demuth and *Fw.* Walter Köhne (20th claim) among the scorers.

Fw. Fritz Haspel, who took off at 10.30 hrs, was the only pilot from III./JG 1 to claim a victory when he accounted for a Thunderbolt near Osnabrück (the American pilot baled out). The last two victories for JG 1 – a B-17 and a P-47 – were claimed at about 13.00 hrs by the *Kommodore*, Walter Oesau.

Fw. Walter Köhne of 3./JG 1 also remembered that day and wrote: "*What a mess today! Once they tell you they are coming and next moment, they don't… The 'sitting' warning is replaced by a 10 minute warning, after which they want you to go and wait in the aircraft until it all starts again. Now you've got a 30 minute warning.*

"*So, we'll be able to go and eat. But then the telephone rings the moment you sit down to table. 'SCRAMBLE!' We leave our plates behind and race to our machines. After a first check up, the Gruppe gets under way: 1. Staffel, the Gruppenstab and then 3. Staffel to bring up the rear. The Focke-Wulfs take off one after the other. However, one of them bangs into the roof of a house and crashes onto the ground with a terrible explosion. The poor Leutnant* (Author's note: Uffz. Lothar Hänert) *will die the next day… What a great start!*

"*I give full throttle as required, fly over the fire and join the Gruppe at grid 'Caruso Ost' heading to the east. Just as in previous days, the weather is so clear that we can immediately see condensation at 7,000 m. Soon afterwards, some fighters make a dive attack towards our group. Our formation breaks up, each of us making a steep turn. What a panic for nothing! It was just some Bf 109s! 'They're our brothers!' I cry out over the radio using fighter pilot jargon. Once again, it is quiet. I see our squadron is now reduced to five aircraft in formation. I keep close to the Kapitän so that he can at least rely on my Schwarm. My number four has disappeared, turned into a smoking crater with just an identification disc somewhere amongst the debris, as I would discover later. What bad luck, indeed today!*

"*The leader flutters his ailerons and points at unidentifiable machines flying at a lower height. My comrades manoeuvred towards the small dots, but I feel a growing pain. I breathe some oxygen in for a long time so as to feel better. As soon as I recover my senses, I realise I am alone with Ossi.* (Author's note: Uffz. Wolf Oswald of 3./JG 1). *He's no exceptional pilot, but he's brave and trustworthy. Both of us know we can rely on each other. At 300 m higher, a Mustang suddenly flies out of the sun straight in front of us. Where are my fellow pilots? I cautiously follow my course in his direction. The P-51 makes a curve so as to place itself behind us. There it is, once again! I turn left. Ossi hasn't noticed anything, yet carelessly follows me. As a matter of fact, his sight isn't that good despite his glasses. The American's position is particularly advantageous. My fellow pilot finally becomes aware of the danger and follows my steep turn. But our pursuer is a formidable pilot and he won't let us go. He slowly draws closer to Ossi. I shout at my friend to make a sharp turn. No use. The American launches his first attack. His aim isn't very well aligned yet, but the fatal moment is drawing closer. I yell – 'Stick full back!'*

"At last, Ossi reacts and stalls his aircraft. The American is surprised and lets him go. Now, he concentrates on my Fw 190. I call Ossi: 'Congratulations! Now climb back and help me!' As we execute manoeuvre after manoeuvre, neither my opponent nor I succeed in placing ourselves in firing range. As I look backwards, I catch sight of Ossi. Dear Ossi! How many would have fled instead of going up again to give a comrade a hand?

"As he notices my comrade approach, the Mustang pilot climbs towards the sun at full throttle and disappears. It seems that everything is going to go wrong today. With Ossi following on my heels, I climb again in search of the Viermots.

"I was beginning to despair when I finally located aircraft over Osnabrück. I catch sight of a Schwarm at the same altitude. But let's be cautious! Are they friends or enemies? They are Fw 190s! We catch up with them and the whole group races towards a large bomber box. But what's happening in front of us? Our leader turns left. We follow in his wake and fly past the four-engined aircraft. God! I hate tail attacks! But an order is an order! Let's do our duty! A new manoeuvre by the leader surprises me once more. Followed by his wingmen, he turns right much too early. This time, I let him slip away and choose the Fortress at the right end of the group. I draw closer and put the rear gunner out of action. I get closer and closer. My shells tear at the wings and destroy the 'giant's' tail unit. Surrounded by tracer-bullets, I stall to the right. I feel a small shock, my wing has been hit but the damage is not serious. Trailing thick black smoke, my Viermot gradually loses height. Ossi seems to have disappeared, yet the sky is full of Allied fighters. Are there no German fighters left? Seeing everything going wrong, I remained cautious. I dive

Lt. Hans Halbey, III./JG 1's Technical Officer, proudly hands over to his Kommandeur, Hptm. Friedrich Eberle, the 500th Bf 109 delivered to the Gruppe, Volkel, 19 February 1944.

to the left to observe my victim's destiny. Though constantly losing height, the bomber changes direction; after heading northwards, he now turns westwards. At least those bombs won't hit their target! The smoke gets thinner and thinner before disappearing at last. They have extinguished the fire on board. I follow the bomber without getting too close because I don't trust the Lightnings and Mustangs ahead of me. Apparently, they hadn't seen me. My bomber heads for a frontal area of clouds 2,500 metres further on. Now, I must close in for the kill, otherwise he might escape me. A shadow catches up with me. I turn and identify an Fw 190. I flutter my wings so as to invite him to follow me. Where is my Viermot now? I just have time enough to fire a burst at him before he enters the cloud. I keep flying at the same height and in the same direction – westwards.

"A little later, I discover a hole in the cloudy mass and guessed that would be where he would reappear. The bomber emerges as I thought. But the pilot sees me and dives back into the smog. This time, I follow him and start firing at it with all my weapons from only a few metres behind him. Strikes register along the fuselage. One of his landing wheels breaks free and falls into the void. The 'giant' is now completely on fire. It dives into a cloud which I turn over and cross. A second later, a flash lights up the sky. The Viermot has just exploded. Followed by my wingman, I fly over the crash site near the canal in Recke, not far from the airfield at Hopsten. Ossi lands a few minutes before I do. He has had his engine damaged by the defensive fire from one of the Americans. Two years later, I would go back to Recke by bicycle, anxious to know more about my victim's destiny. I would then hear that nine crewmen had been able to escape the burning aircraft. As I didn't see any parachutes, I guess they baled out while passing through the cloud, a few seconds before the explosion."

On 19 February 1944, the Allies launched their massive, week-long, aerial offensive, Operation Argument, code named 'Big Week', designed to paralyse the German aircraft manufacturing industry. During 'Big Week' nearly 20,000 tons of bombs were dropped on the Reich, principally on aircraft factories.

On 20 February, the three *Gruppen* of JG 1 were in action against a wave of 1,000 bombers escorted by 17 squadrons of American fighters and 16 British. Twenty Fw 190 A-6s and A-7s made three passes against the bombers. The third, at about 13.30 hrs in the region of Magdeburg, was the most effective with *Ofw.* Reinhard Flecks claiming a *Herausschuss* and a P-38, while four other victories (three B-17s and one P-38), were claimed by II. *Gruppe*. I. *Gruppe* was also deployed, *Ofw.* Demuth claiming a B-17 and *Oblt.* Ehlers a P-51. But 2. *Staffel* lost its *Staffelkapitän*, *Hptm.* Harald Römer. His place was taken by a veteran of JG 54, *Oblt.* Helmut Biederbick, who recalled: "I was on the Eastern Front with JG 54 when victories were still relatively easy… Even less a problem for others, because I myself was not an aggressive pilot at heart; I was too concerned about watching my rear, and did not concentrate enough on my prey.

"I was posted to Schleissheim as an instructor, and from there to Manching, where I met Harald Römer. Römer left us to return to the front – he was posted to JG 1. He could not have served long in his role as *Staffelkapitän* because soon, to avoid a court-martial following several pranks, I in turn had to return to action and learned unfortunately that the *Staffel* I had been given was that of my friend Harald, who had fallen shortly beforehand. The *Reichsverteidigung* was a terrible period. The Eastern Front, which I had known, was far less dangerous. In the case of an alert in the west, we usually had five minutes to prepare ourselves, put on the obligatory life jacket

Oblt. Helmut Biederbick, an experienced Eastern Front pilot from JG 54, replaced his friend, Hptm. Harald Römer, as Staffelkapitän of 2./JG 1 on 20 February 1944. He is seen in his Fw 190 A-7 'Black 7' which has been fitted with flame dampers.

Major Heinz Bär visits the wreckage of B-17 F 'Miss Ouachita' of the 91st Bomb Group which he shot down on 21 February 1944. He is accompanied by his two usual wingmen: Ofw. Leo Schuhmacher (wearing a prized American flying jacket) and Fw. Max Sauer (killed on 29 March 1944). Bär insisted on the fact that his wingmen were sufficiently experienced to be able to lead the Gruppe themselves in case of his absence.

"To do our duty, even unto death..." 215

and go to the toilet as nerves took a hold. Loudspeakers blared out military marches. We would gather near our aircraft, accompanied by the music which was sometimes interrupted by news concerning the advance of the 'Dicke Autos' or 'Indianer'. We followed their progress on a map. Each *Staffelkapitän* had a telephone on the wing of his aircraft linked to the *Stab* section. The music was interrupted when it came to *Sitzbereitschaft* – cockpit readiness. At any moment we could be taking off. A green flare over the airfield was the signal; engines would be started and we would take off. When the enemy was sighted, we flew for several seconds parallel to the formation in order to evaluate its strength and direction. We were aware of the escort fighters, but often they did not attack at that particular moment. We picked up speed, swept wide of our target, and carried out a 180 degree turn. We were then head-on, and opened fire while traversing through the bomber stream. During this move, our formation lost cohesion, and that was what the enemy fighters were waiting for. They then picked us off at the rear of the *Viermots*."

On 21 February, the cities of Braunschweig and Hannover, as well as about 15 aircraft plants in central Germany, were the focus of attention for 861 bombers of the Eighth Air Force. Sixteen of them were shot down, of which four were claimed by II./JG 1 plus two *Herauschüsse*. *Major* Bär claimed three victories and a *Herausschuss*, taking his personal tally to 185. *Oblt*. von Kirchmayr claimed a *Herausschuss* and the official leader of II. *Gruppe*, *Hptm*. Hermann Segatz, a victory over a B-24. On the debit side, the *Gruppe* lost two pilots killed and three wounded, *Fw*. Otto Schmid, with seven victories, of which five were *Viermots*, among the latter. He managed to get his Fw 190 A-7 down at Rheine in spite of a bad wound to his leg. Having received the distress message from the pilot, the airfield commander fired a red flare to prevent other aircraft from landing. Medical services were with him immediately he landed, but in spite of all assistance, Schmid's leg had to be amputated in June.

The aircraft of III./JG 1, which had taken off shortly after 15.00 hrs, were bounced by P-47s coming out of the sun. Two pilots were killed. *Fw*. Fritz Haspel, piloting a Bf 109 G-6 of 8. *Staffel,* had been unable to release his auxiliary fuel tank before going into attack and lost contact with his formation. Suddenly his aircraft received a burst of fire in the engine from a P-47. Haspel immediately began the procedure for a crash-landing. A second burst hit his machine. This time, there was no question of a crash-landing – he had to bale out. Haspel jumped after jettisoning the canopy. The latter hit the propeller of the Thunderbolt and it, in turn, went down out of control. The American pilot managed to bale out but, deploying his parachute too quickly, the silk tore, and he broke both legs due to his rapid descent. Haspel was credited with the victory, but he suffered second degree burns to his face which required four weeks of treatment. His *Staffel* comrade, *Ofhr*. Erich Zulauf was luckier; he opened his tally by shooting down a B-17 and returned without problem. Haspel was not the only III. *Gruppe* loss; two other pilots were killed.

The following day, it was the turn of aircraft production facilities in central Germany and the industrial region of Schweinfurt to suffer attack. The whole of JG 1 found itself in action. II. *Gruppe* shot down five B-17s and claimed three *Herausschüsse*. Among the successful pilots were the usual two 'aces', *Major* Bär and *Hptm*. Segatz, who claimed a B-17 and a *Herausschuss*. With two victories accredited to *Ofw*. Rudolf Hübl and *Oblt*. Hans Ehlers, I. *Gruppe's* score was more modest and equalled the accomplishments of the *Geschwaderstab* where Walter Oesau claimed two further B-17s.

However, the constant onslaught was beginning to take its toll on the *Jagdwaffe*. In a telling comment, the US Eighth Air Force stated that *"... enemy air opposition, as on the previous day's mission, was remarkably weak considering the depth of penetration and the importance to the Luftwaffe of targets attacked."*

On 23 February, the US Fifteenth Air Force, operating from bases in Italy, entered the fray with targets in Steyr, Austria as its objective. By and large, north-west and central Europe enjoyed a day of peace from the bombers.

On 24 February, I./JG 1 intercepted 809 bombers over Holland en route for Rostock, Schweinfurt, Gotha and Eisenach. The *Gruppe* claimed the destruction of five B-24s, two downed by *Ofw*. Rudolf Hübl and the others by *Ofw*. Anton Piffer, *Ofw*. Emil Demuth and the *Gruppenkommandeur,* Emil Schnoor. I. *Gruppe*, however, lost three pilots killed and one wounded.

At about 12.15 hrs, a few minutes before launching an attack against the bombers, II./JG 1 was disturbed by the intervention of about 15 P-47 escort fighters. The *Gruppe* had to change course, but Bär succeeded in reorganising his unit before launching a second attack in close formation. This time, it was to prove successful. Bär claimed two B-24s while *Oblt*. von Kirchmayr and two other pilots each claimed one. Two P-47s would have also been claimed, but their final destruction went unobserved. However, the *Gruppe* suffered three pilots killed, among them the experienced *Fw*. Heinz Fuchs of 4. *Staffel*. The *Geschwaderstab* attacked together with II./JG 1 and Walter Oesau again accounted for one B-17. The III. *Gruppe* was in action towards 14.30 hrs. The *Gruppe* Technical Officer, *Lt*. Hans Halbey, scored his first victory over a P-47 at 9,000 m (29,527 ft). It was III. *Gruppe's* only victory that day.

On 25 February, the unit once more engaged the Americans as they concluded the 'Big Week' offensive, this time with a force of 754 bombers escorted by 899 fighters heading for targets in southern Germany. All JG 1's pilots survived the attack and the *Geschwader* claimed no fewer than 11 *Viermots,* five of which were classified as *Herausschuss.* Heinz Bär was again victorious; in his first engagement, he downed a B-17 and claimed another as a *Herausschüsse.* He landed, rested, refuelled and then took off again. Another B-24 fell to his guns, and he was credited with a further *Herausschuss.* Walter Oesau also increased his score by claims for a B-17 and a B-24 in two missions

Uffz. Walter Pleines from 7./JG 1 shot down a B-17 representing the sole *Abschuss* for III./JG 1. He remembers: "On 25 February 1944, our III. *Gruppe* took off around midday from Volkel airfield on a southerly course. Before taking off, all pilots had received the order to land on our new airfield at München-Gladbach following completion of the mission. In 7. *Staffel*, I flew as 'Y-Lotse' (radio-guide) and we gained altitude immediately. After a short time, we saw to our left our 'little brothers' from I. and II./JG 1. Our radio continuously kept us informed of the enemy's course; bombers and escort fighters had crossed the Channel and were over the French-Belgian border... We flew roughly parallel to the Rhine in the direction of Frankfurt. We had reached 6,000 metres and saw the enemy formation over the Main. Seeing no escort fighters, I immediately attacked a B-17 from the rear and observed several hits on the target. The bomber's pilot immediately turned right towards Switzerland. During my second attack, my right wing was also hit and I had to interrupt my approach. Nevertheless, I came back for a third time and saw that one of the crew members had already left the aircraft and was hanging by his parachute. The B-17 crashed in the Heilbronn area. The witness was *Ofw.* Thies. Having no sight of the ground and flying over a large cloudy area, I informed the ground of my victory and my situation. Thanks to my aircraft's radio equipment, I received from the ground my exact position with *Planquadrat* data. After a short stay at Rhein-Main airfield in order to refuel, I took off again and landed at around 15.00 hours at München-Gladbach."

The Allies paid a heavy price for the 'Big Week' missions; 160 four-engined bombers were claimed shot down by German fighters. Furthermore, although substantial damage had been inflicted to the German aircraft production industry, final results were far below Allied hopes. German production was slowed for a few weeks, but by late March 1944, the factories were back in full working order.

February had been an extremely hard month for the *Jagdwaffe* with about 240 pilots killed (29 from JG 1) and 140 wounded (11 from JG 1).

On 1 March 1944, *Oblt.* Burath took charge of 4. *Staffel*. In spite of the impressive number of victories registered by the unit, he noted with sadness that over three months of action, 36 pilots had passed through the *Staffel* – three times normal strength.

LEFT: *In February 1944, Hptm. and Ritterkreuzträger Lutz-Wilhelm Burkhardt (right) became Staffelkapitän of 7./JG 1. He converses at Paderborn with his Kommandeur, Hptm. Friedrich Eberle in front of a Bf 109 G-6/AS fitted with an 'Erla Haube' canopy.*

BELOW: *Of these ten pilots from 1./JG 1 photographed at Hopsten at the end of February 1944, only two are 'veterans': Lt. Heinz-Günther Lück and Fw. Erich Kaiser. From left to right: Uffz. Kubon (killed 29 March 1944), Uffz. Altenhain, Uffz. Manikowski (killed 11 April 1944), Uffz. Kenzler, Uffz. Martin (killed 29 March 1944), Uffz. Schulze, Lt. Lück (injured 9 April 1944), Uffz. Talbat, Fjfw Junge (injured 14 August 1944) and Fw. Kaiser. In the background is Fw 190 A-7 'White 17'.*

Fw 190 A-7 'Black 3' of 2./JG 1 (W.Nr. 430352) takes off from a snow-covered runway. The aircraft is fitted with an auxiliary fuel tank.

Focke-Wulf Fw 190 A-7 W.Nr. 430352
'Black 3'
2./JG 1
Dortmund
January 1944

ABOVE: *Fw 190 A-7 'Black 3' (W.Nr. 430352) of 2./JG 1 at Dortmund, January 1944. This aircraft carries the black and white bands on the cowling with the new unit emblem (only on the left side), as well as the large red Defence of the Reich band on the rear fuselage. Note that the Black '3' is outlined with a narrow red band.*

RIGHT: *This Fw 190 A-7 of Stab I./JG 1 shows clearly the lack of continuation of the black and white bands onto the lower engine cowling. Note the armoured windshield as well as the window for the 'Schießkamera' - gun camera - between the wing-mounted weapons.*

"To do our duty, even unto death..." **219**

ABOVE: Groundcrew of I./JG 1 line up for orders in a hangar at Dortmund, early 1944. In the background is a Fw 190 carrying black and white cowling bands.

RIGHT: Armourers feed ammunition into the wing-mounted MG 151/20 of an Fw 190 A-7 of I./JG 1.

BELOW: In a flurry of snow-spray, Fw 190 A-6s of I./JG 1 take off wingtip-to-wingtip from Dortmund, early 1944.

220 JG 1 – Defenders of the Reich

RIGHT: A Fw 190 A-6 of I./JG 1 runs up its engines outside one of the hangars at Dortmund, early 1944.

LEFT: Fw 190 A-7 'Yellow 6' (W.Nr. 340283) of 3./JG 1 undergoing refuelling. The aircraft carries the Defence of the Reich markings, but without the Geschwader emblem on the right side of the engine cowling. This aircraft was lost on 8 February 1944 when Fw. Gerhard Giese of 3./JG 1 was killed during combat operations against heavy bombers.

Focke-Wulf Fw 190 A-7 W.Nr. 340283 'Yellow 6'
3./JG 1
late 1943/early 1944

"To do our duty, even unto death..." **221**

BELOW: Rheine, early 1944; II./JG 1 had shared its Fw 190s with II./JG 300 since the summer of the previous year. This Fw 190 A-6 carried the winged '1' and is about to take-off on a 'Wilde Sau' mission with the latter unit.

ABOVE: Ofw. Otto Bach of 5./JG 1 climbs out of his Fw 190 A-7 at Rheine, early 1944. Note the flame dampers over the engine-mounted machine guns.

LEFT: Supplementary fuel tanks were fitted and then filled (as shown here) before take-off for operations against American bomber formations. 1st Wart Konrad 'Kari' Ell is working on the BMW 801 D-2 engine of this Fw 190 A-7 of 1./JG 1 as the the aircraft is refuelled. Note the 'Panzer Ölkühler' – armoured oil cooler.

**Focke-Wulf Fw 190 A-7 'White 9'
Hptm. Alfred Grislawski,
1./JG 1
early 1944**

Hptm. Alfred Grislawski stands on the wing of his Fw 190 A-7 'White 9'. There are several interesting points to note: the flame dampers over the engine-mounted 13 mm machine guns (this aircraft was enhanced in order to fly night operations), the armoured windscreen (typical windshield for a Sturmgruppe aircraft), the Pitot tube at the tip of the right wing (characteristic of the Fw 190 A-8 with which JG 1 would be progressively equipped from April 1944), and last but not least, the red Defence of the Reich band and lower engine cowling panel. A very typical aircraft! Standing on the fuselage is Ogefr. Josef Peters.

"To do our duty, even unto death…" **223**

LEFT: *An in-flight view of a Schwarm of 3./JG 1, early 1944.*

RIGHT: *From 12 to 24 February 1944, I./JG 1 occupied Rheine-Hopsten airfield. With battery charger plugged in and opened cockpits, these three aircraft are at readiness.*

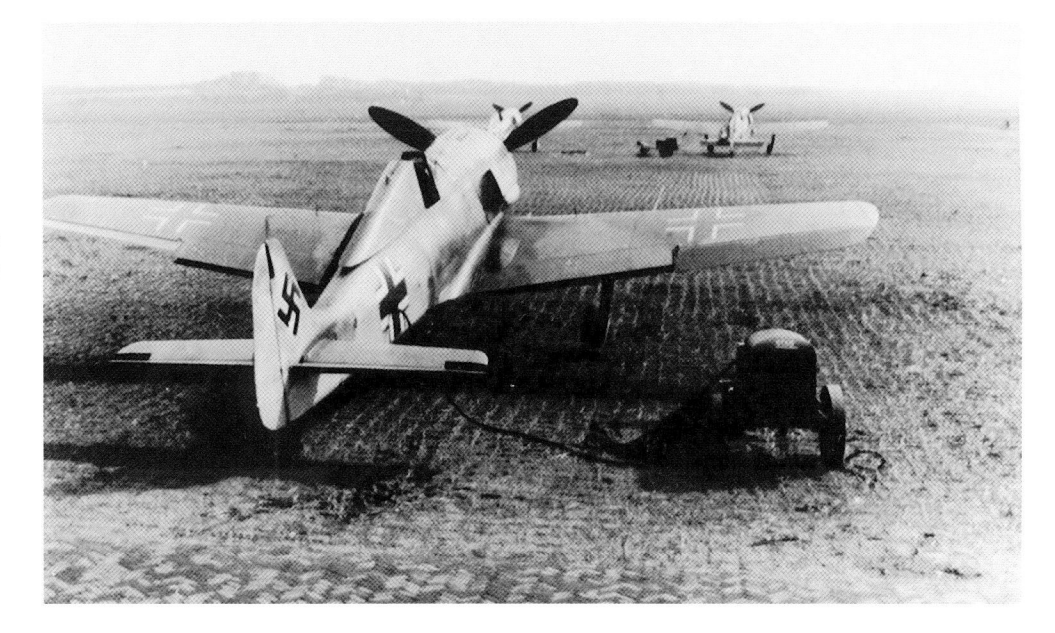

BELOW: *Fw. Walter Köhne's Fw 190 A crashed during take-off at Hopsten, in February/March 1944. The pilot, from 3./JG 1, was unhurt.*

ABOVE: *Eight pilots from 3./JG 1 pose for a snapshot in front of Fw 190 A-7 'Yellow 12' (W.Nr. 340031) at Hopsten. From left to right: Uffz. Oswald, Hptm. Wrobel, Uffz. Rühl, Uffz. Enderle, Uffz. Kirchhoff, Uffz. Finger, Lt. Eh and Fw. Köhne.*

224 JG 1 – Defenders of the Reich

Some time during February-March 1944, Fw 190 A-7 (W.Nr. 340268) 'White 8' of 4./JG 1, made a wheels-up landing near Mulhouse, in the Alsace, France. Note the spiral spinner, the JG 1 emblem, red fuselage band and II. Gruppe horizontal bar. This aircraft was lost in combat on 8 April 1944 with Uffz. Heinz Eberl of 4./JG 1 at the controls.

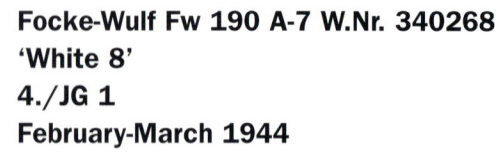

Focke-Wulf Fw 190 A-7 W.Nr. 340268
'White 8'
4./JG 1
February-March 1944

Chapter Seventeen

Berlin Debut

In the opinion of Winston Churchill, the 1,600 kilometres (1,000 mls) which separated Berlin from Great Britain were no longer an obstacle to the might and capability of Allied airpower. The British leader once prophesised: "For every bomb dropped on England, we will repay with a thousand." The reality however, was that the capital of the Reich – or 'Big B' as the Americans called it – had not, as yet, been seriously affected by daylight bombing. Hermann Göring, for his part, bragged that if Berlin ever suffered bombardment again, then the people would be justified in labelling him with the humble name of "Meier". As events would prove, this was a wholly unwise boast on the part of the over-confident *Reichsmarschall*.

Jagdgeschwader 1 formed part of 3. *Jagddivision*, under the command of *Generalmajor* Walter Grabmann, based at Deelen.

On 6 March 1944, JG 1 was composed as follows:

Stab   *Oberst* Walter Oesau with three Bf 109 G-6s based at Rheine
I. Gruppe   *Major* Emil-Rudolf Schnoor with 19 Fw 190 A-7s based at Twente
II. Gruppe *Hptm.* Hermann Segatz with 21 Fw 190 A-5 and A-7s based at Rheine
III. Gruppe *Hptm.* Friedrich Eberle with 13 Bf 109 G-5 and G-6s based at München-Gladbach.

Since dawn on 6 March, intense preparations were being made at the British bases of the US Eighth Air Force in readiness, in a just few hours time, to take the war in the air to a new dimension. A force of 730 bombers were slated to take part in that day's forthcoming mission and they would be escorted by 801 fighters.

At 08.50 hrs, the first aircraft took off. From that moment, the German radar listening services were continually tuned into the Eighth Air Force's 250th bombing mission. More than an hour before the first American aircraft crossed the Channel, preparatory orders had been issued to the German fighter units. For this attack, the units of 2. and 3. *Jagddivision* would work closely together under the tactical directorship of the *Gruppenkommandeur* of I./JG 11, *Hptm.* Rolf Hermichen. This policy had been successfully put to the test several days earlier over the Steinhuder Lake and allowed concentration of a sizeable force with which to strike against the American heavies.

The first Boeings reached the coast of Holland at 10.52 hrs. With engines running at cruising speed to conserve fuel, the escort fighters slowly made up the distance between themselves and their charges.

At last, the interminable *Sitzbereitschaft* (cockpit readiness) came to an end on the majority of *Luftwaffe* fighter bases across western Europe. At Twente, *Major* Schnoor's I. *Gruppe* took off at 10.55 hrs, setting course for the Steinhuder Lake. I. *Gruppe* was joined over Rheine by the 21 Fw 190s of II./JG 1, led by *Major* Heinz Bär. The two *Gruppen* were the last to arrive over the Lake, meeting up with 50 Bf 109s and Fw 190s from JG 11 and 20 Bf 109s of III./JG 54. JG 1's arrival meant that a force of more than 100 fighters would go into action, a force which far exceeded the usual German strike capability. For the first time in a long time, the young German pilots experienced a feeling of invulnerability. However, their numbers could still not compare with those put into the fray by the Americans.

A scene in II./JG 1's operations room at Rheine in March 1944. Hptm. Hermann Segatz (centre) had been appointed Kommandeur of the Gruppe some two weeks earlier. Seated at the table is Oblt. Eberhard Burath, Staffelkapitän of 4./JG 1.

BELOW: *Five pilots of I./JG 1 at Dortmund, early 1944: (from left) Ofw. Anton Piffer, Lt. Herbert Eh, Lt. Hans Berger, Hptm. Emil-Rudolf Schnoor and Lt. Hans Ehlers.*

At 11.40 hrs, the German formation set course to the west and the hunt began. The advantage lay with those who spotted the enemy first. Suddenly, silhouettes appeared in the distance. As a result of instrument failure, part of the American force – the 1st and 3rd Bomb Divisions – deviated to the south. Realising their error, the American navigators corrected their course to the north, unaware that this correction would help them avoid enemy fighters. The second bomber formation had less luck. It found itself among the German fighters. Targets were chosen. The German fighters pounced. At that moment the bombers could only rely on the quality of their gunners and their defensive armament for they had to endure the force of this first frontal attack without their escort. However, the frontal pass would also break up the German formation and it would be far less dangerous thereafter. The German fighter pilots tensed; there was perspiration on every brow. *Hptm.* Rolf Hermichen gave the order to attack.

The first blazing victims fell away from the formation. The debris of around ten Flying Fortresses fell in the Quackenbrück area. But it was then the turn of the German fighters to become boxed in, as, slowly but surely, the escort reacted. One of the first victims was the Fw 190 A-7 of *Oblt.* Wolfgang Kretschmer (recently arrived from JG 54) who lost contact with the rest of II. *Gruppe* after probably having shot down a *Viermot* during the frontal attack. Alone, he was preparing for a second attack from the rear. At full throttle, Colonel 'Hub' Zemke, commander of the 56th Fighter Group, flew his P-47s towards Kretschmer. The latter realised the gravity of his situation too late, and despite his frantic evasive manoeuvres, Kretschmer could not escape. The American opened fire. The Focke-Wulf's fuselage was hit and the aircraft began to break up and burn. Kretschmer had to get out quickly before the fuel tank exploded. Blinded by the flames, deafened by the noise around him, he managed to extricate himself with difficulty from the spiralling inferno. Finally clear, the shock of the parachute opening brought home to him that he was still alive. He was later found on the ground, his face, hands and clothing all ravaged by flames. An ambulance took him away for treatment and he subsequently spent ten weeks in convalescence in Quackenbrück. High above, the action continued.

Fhj.Ofw. Emil Demuth of 3./JG 1 suffered a similar fate to Kretschmer. "At the beginning of March 1944, my *Kommodore,* Oesau, called me to talk over a problem concerning an officer in my *Staffel. Lt.* W. had been in the unit for some weeks, but he had not lodged any claims. On every occasion, he had interrupted his combat mission for 'technical' reasons in spite of the fact that his aircraft was always OK. Oesau told me: '*Demuth, on the next mission, you take W. as your wingman, and you oblige him to conduct the whole mission with you.*' I went to *Lt.* W. and told him of the *Kommodore's* orders. On 6 March, he took off after me, as my *Rottenflieger.* Already, while the *Gruppe* was climbing towards the bombers, I saw that *Lt.* W. did not maintain tight formation and I called him twice over the radio, ordering him to close in on my wings. After shooting down a B-17 during my first attack, I placed a second Boeing in my gun-sight. But just before I went in for the attack, I looked towards the rear and saw that my wingman had disappeared. I saw him flying below me. I ordered my men to continue with the attack, interrupted my own attack and dived in his direction. I caught him up easily, cut into him and ordered him once again to stay with me, threatening him. We had begun again to climb when I sighted five P-47s above us. They were not long in turning towards our own direction so as to adopt a good attack position. I warned my wingman and looked behind to verify his position. I was not that surprised to see that he had disappeared once again.

"My Fw 190 was hit in the fuselage and in the wings. It caught fire immediately. There was only one thing to do – bale out quickly! I released my harness and jettisoned the canopy. The sudden ensuing rush of air threw the flames towards my face and I instinctively brought my hands up to my eyes. With my foot, I pushed the stick forward and let myself drift out into the slipstream. My flying-suit, my boots and my gloves were still burning. I twisted and wriggled in an attempt to extinguish the flames, but in vain. A glance downwards made me realise with horror that it was high time to open the parachute which I did with a sharp pull! *Open*! Sparks kept on flickering on my clothes. I was really hoping they wouldn't spread to the silk of my parachute! I fought them as much as I could and I finally managed to put them out.

"I eventually landed close to a village. Three young women arrived on their bicycles and helped me get out of the parachute before taking me to the village. Luckily enough, a military ambulance was stationed there. They smeared me with ointment. My burns were serious – second and third degree to my face and to my hands The ambulance raced towards Minden hospital from where I called my *Stab.*

"Soon afterwards, they came to fetch me. My *Kommodore, Oberst* Oesau called me. '*Demuth, I've contacted my former unit based in Italy so that they could send us a drum of olive oil. Make sure your burns are always moistened with oil and you'll see you won't get scars. I wish you a quick and thorough recovery.*' Indeed, next morning, a motorbike dispatch rider delivered the precious liquid to the hospital. Even today, I feel especially grateful to my *Kommodore* who saved me from the awful after-effects of the burns to my face. When I came back to the unit, someone told me that *Lt. W.* had been posted to the Eastern Front to a disciplinary unit."

The bomber stream approached Berlin. The German fighters were now running short of ammunition and fuel. They had to get down quickly. Of the 21 Fw 190s of II./JG 1 which took off, only two managed to regain their home base. Seventeen others landed at various aerodromes across north-west Germany. Apart from the loss of *Oblt.* Kretschmer, II. *Gruppe* also lost the experienced and highly respected *Ofw.* Detlev Lüth, who remained trapped in his aircraft when it crashed at Eydelstadt.

Jagdgeschwader 1's score for the day was most gratifying – a total of 26 claims: 23 B-17s shot down, one *Herausschuss*, one P-51 and one P-47. The insatiable Bär downed two B-17s during a first mission, and a third during a following sortie. *Uffz.* Helmut Stiegler of 4./JG 1 who flew with Bär, opened his tally with two B-17s, one on each mission. *Hptm.* Hermann Segatz shot down two B-17s in two minutes and the *Kommodore*, Walter Oesau, the P-47 and a B-17 15 minutes later; *Oblt.* Rüdiger von Kirchmayr claimed a B-17 and the P-51; *Fw.* Walter Köhne, two B-17s. Other well-known pilots were also victorious: *Ofw.* Otto Bach, (one B-17), *Uffz.* Hubert Swoboda (one B-17) and Bär's wingman, *Ofw.* Leo Schuhmacher (one B-17), *Lt.* Hans Berger (one B-17) and *Ofw.* Rudolf Hübl (one B-17).

Other units took up the attack and more bombers were sent down. Berlin's air raid warning sirens sounded at 12.47 hrs. Thirteen minutes later, the surviving bombers appeared over the capital, dropping 1,200 tonnes of bombs. A total of 345 civilians were killed.

In England, there was the habitual waiting and worrying on the airfields. The survivors appeared, eventually, and a count was made of missing aircraft. Eighty machines did not return – 69 bombers and 11 fighters.

The run of victories eventually came to an end for one of the 'aces' of II. *Gruppe*. Having recovered from the action of two days before, 21 pilots of II. *Gruppe* took off on 8 March at midday. The Focke-Wulfs met up with the enemy 45 minutes later. The pilots took ten minutes to assess the situation and to manoeuvre into position, then they attacked. Seven victories were returned by pilots of II./JG 1, among them *Uffz.* Stiegler, (a P-47) and three *Herausschüsse* including a B-24 for *Hptm.* Segatz. Nevertheless, Segatz's victim was to be his last. The *Gruppenkommandeur* of II./JG 1 was shot down and killed in his Fw 190 A-7, 'White 23' over Luckau by an American fighter. Segatz had at least 34 victories to his credit. *Oblt.* Edgar Witzmann and *Uffz.* Anton Krampert of 6./JG 1 were also killed during the air combat, while one of the most experienced pilots of this *Staffel*, *Ofw.* Reinhard Flecks, was forced to bale out.

I. *Gruppe* was also successful with five claims, three P-47s going to *Lt.* Ehlers, *Fw.* Hübl and *Fw.* Köhne. III./JG 1 claimed only one victory, a B-17 by *Uffz.* Pleines of 7./JG 1, his second victory.

Heinz Bär, who did not participate in this operation, officially took command of the *Gruppe* the next day. His 6./JG 1 was taken over by *Oblt.* Georg-Peter 'Schorsch' Eder who held the *Deutsches Kreuz* in Gold (a decoration which usually preceded the *Ritterkreuz*), and by this point in time, counted about 30 victories to his credit.

Oblt. Eberhard Burath, *Staffelkapitän* of 4./JG 1 recalls: "Shortly after taking over the *Gruppe*, *Major* Bär wanted us to change our ideas. We were totally exhausted with combat. On the occasion of

ABOVE: *"After Lüth's death, we felt all orphans!"* remembered Fritz Wegner. *Ofw. Detlev Lüth, a II./JG 1 'veteran', was killed in action on 6 March 1944.*

LEFT: *On 6 March 1944, Lt. Hans Berger of 1./JG 1 took off from Twente to intercept the first large-scale American raid on Berlin. He shot down a B-17, but his Fw 190 A-7 'White 3' (W.Nr. 340016) was hit. Nevertheless, he was able to return to Twente. His mechanic, Konrad 'Kari' Ell stands with him near the damaged rudder. This aircraft was handed over to a school unit (2./JG 105) and was 50 per cent damaged on 31 July in a collision.*

After Hptm. Hermann Segatz's death on 8 March 1944, Major Heinz Bär officially took over II. Gruppe. He is seen here at Rheine in March 1944 briefing his pilots (who seemed to be dressed in a somewhat varied manner). From left to right: Oblt. von Kirchmayr, Oblt. Burath, unknown, Lt. Schwarz, Lt. Wegner, Lt. Deppe, Lt. Terborg, Ofw. Bach, Ofw. Schuhmacher, Ofw. Niedereichholz, Fw. Sauer, Fw. Fuchs, Uffz. Zinkl. Ofw. Hutter and Kirchner are also in the line-up.

Many consider that Major Bär (centre) was the best Gruppenführer in the Luftwaffe. If the quality of his vision was excellent, his experience as a hunter (something he developed at a young age) was also a crucial factor. Here he discusses tactics with a superior officer. To his left is Oblt. Rüdiger von Kirchmayr and, second from right, Ofw. Otto Bach.

a transfer of base, he took us to dine in the best restaurant in Wiesbaden. We were fairly embarrassed following him into the main room. What would people think? Our leaders had said we were slovenly, incapable. Also, a few days before, the city had suffered a heavy raid which we were unable to prevent. Would we also be insulted here? A great surprise awaited us. First of all there was silence, then applause! A feeling of pride came over us. There were still people who recognised the sacrifices we made. The service was exemplary, and we ate with the civilians. The last glass was emptied late into the night."

For the rest of March, JG 1 would only be involved in two major operations against the bombers; on 23rd, the *Geschwader* – principally II. *Gruppe* – claimed eight B-17s, damaged another and shot down a P-47 for the loss of one pilot, *Uffz.* Johann Röhl of 3./JG 1 and several aircraft damaged. On 29th, *Major* Bär (two P-51s) *Uffz.* Stiegler (one P-51), *Oblt.* von Kirchmayr (one B-17) and *Oblt.* Ehlers proved dangerous opponents for the Allied fighter escort. Nevertheless, the German victories on this day were gained at a high price: I. *Gruppe* lost six pilots killed and II. *Gruppe*, two, including *Fhj-Fw.* Max Sauer of the *Gruppenstab*.

On 8 April, the Eighth Air Force launched raids on several airfields in north-west Germany, as well as against aircraft factories in Braunschweig. Once again, the assigned forces involved were enormous – 664 bombers escorted by 780 fighters. At 12.55 hrs, 36 Fw 190s of II./JG 1 took off from Störmede, their new base. Joined by I. and III. *Gruppen* over Paderborn, they established contact with the *Viermots* one hour later. Bär was first at the enemy. I. and II./JG 1 claimed 17 victories (among them five B-24s for 6./JG 1 alone). Several pilots from II./JG 1 were victorious: *Major* Bär, *Ofw.* Schuhmacher, *Ofw.* Bach, *Uffz.* Stiegler, *Oblt.* von Kirchmayr and *Oblt.* Eder who scored his first 'kill' with JG 1 (one B-24 – the first in a long series). In I./JG 1 the victors included *Oblt.* Ehlers, *Fw.* Köhne, *Oblt.* Biederbick (one B-24 *Herausschuss* and one P-51) and *Fw.* Piffer. The latter two pilots were also shot down but escaped by parachute. JG 1 lost two pilots killed, *Uffz.* Johann Pomperger of 3./JG 1 and *Uffz.* Heinz Eberl of 4./JG 1.

On 9 April, *Oblt.* Eder claimed two more victories (one B-24 and a P-47, his 35th and 36th victories) following a joint frontal attack by JG 1 and

I./JG 11 against American bombers attacking more aircraft production targets in northern and central Germany. JG 1 claimed 13 victories (among them five *Herausschüsse*). This time, III. *Gruppe* was also able to claim several enemy aircraft destroyed: one P-47 for *Hptm.* Lutz-Wilhelm Burkhardt, *Kapitän* of 7./JG 1 (his 60th *Abschuss*), a B-17 for *Lt.* Franz Koplik of 9./JG 1, which opened his account, and two B-17s for *Hptm.* Alfred Grislawski (122 and 123). The latter had just returned to the unit to take over 8./JG 1 having suffered wounds in January 1944. This mission saw three JG 1 pilots killed: *Ogfr.* Martin Finger (3./JG 1), *Lt.* Meinhard Quack (4./JG 1) and *Uffz.* Günter Koch (7./JG 1). Two pilots were wounded.

During an operation launched on the 11th, the planned joint tactical grouping of JG 1 and JG 27 failed. Nevertheless, JG 1 scored 13 B-17s, among them two *Herausschüsse*, 5 P-51s, three P-47s and 1 B-24. Several names cropped up again as successful pilots; *Oblt.* Ehlers (one B-17 and two P-51s), *Major* Schnoor (two B-17s), *Ofw.* Kaiser (two P-47s), *Major* Bär (Fw 190 A-7, 'Red 23'), *Ofw.* Schuhmacher (Fw 190 A-7, 'Red 22'), *Oblt.* Eder (Fw 190 A-7, 'Yellow 4'), *Ofw.* Bach (Fw 190 A-7 'Black 2'), *Oblt.* Burath and *Oblt.* Engleder who had returned to JG 1 having suffered wounds in December 1943. He would not stay with the unit long however, being transferred away several days later. However, these victories cost five killed and three wounded from the *Geschwader*.

Despite lack of German tactical co-ordination, the Eighth Air Force post-mission report recorded that "... *the enemy continued one of his most severe and well co-ordinated defences marked by the skilful handling of a considerable number of single-engine fighters in the Hannover-Oschersleben area.*"

Maintaining their conviction in spite of recent heavy losses, the Americans came back on 13 April 1944 to hit various targets in southern Germany, including Schweinfurt. A 'welcoming party' from JG 1 resulted in 13 victories (eight B-17s, two P-51s, two B-24s and one P-47). *Uffz.* Hubert Swoboda of 5./JG 1 performed well once again. After having joined I. and III. *Gruppen* over Paderborn at about 13.00 hrs, his II. *Gruppe* faced a formation of 50 B-17s at 6,500 m (21,325 ft). The large number of P-47 Thunderbolts prevented II./JG 1 from destroying more than two B-17s, accredited to *Oblt.* Eder (Fw 190 A-7, 'Yellow 4') and *Uffz.* Swoboda. The latter was flying a Fw 190 A-7/R-2 ('Black 4'), which was equipped with two fearsome 30 mm MK 108 cannon reinforcing the usual armament. Following his victory, Swoboda landed at Wiesbaden. Rested, he took off again at 15.05 hrs, joining another unit. With his comrades, he caught up with a group of 200 B-17s returning to England from a raid on Augsburg.

LEFT: *Oblt. Schüller of 6./JG 1 climbs out of his Fw 190 'Yellow 3' at Störmede on 8 April 1944 following his first victory over a B-24.*

BELOW LEFT AND BELOW: *Two photographs showing Ofw. Otto Bach of 5./JG 1. (BELOW LEFT) Bach is seen with his two mechanics in front of his Fw 190 which bears the winged '1' emblem of Jagdgeschwader 1. On 8 and 11 April 1944, Bach claimed the destruction of a B-24 Liberator and B-17 Flying Fortress respectively. (BELOW) Bach is greeted by members of the groundcrew following the return from another mission.*

ABOVE: On 11 April 1944, while JG 1 was in action against American heavy bombers, Hptm. Alfred Grislawski of III./JG 1 received the Eichenlaube at Hitler's headquarters. He was accompanied by other fighter aces; from right to left, Lt. Günther Schack, Oblt. Emil Lang, Major Erich Rudorffer, Major Martin Möbus, Major Wilhelm Herget and an unknown officer.

BELOW AND BELOW RIGHT: On 16 April 1944, Hptm. Schnoor, Gruppenkommandeur of I./JG 1, took off on a routine flight. Shortly afterwards, his Fw 190 A-7 'White 20' (W.Nr. 340035) crashed near Detmold. Badly wounded, Schnoor handed command of his Gruppe to Oblt. Hans Ehlers, formerly 3./JG 1.

Swoboda attacked from the rear, aiming at the last bomber to the right of the formation. The fire from the 30 mm cannon shook the Fw 190, and the damage inflicted to the bomber was terrible; the left wing became just a sheet of shredded metal and the tail rudder disappeared. Three airmen parachuted out, while Swoboda, firing all his guns, was only two to three metres (6.5-10 ft) from the giant. Suddenly, the bomber veered to the left and disappeared. Swoboda's Focke-Wulf suddenly shook again but this time from enemy fire. His aircraft burst into flames and with his head slightly burned, he was able to jump out with his parachute at the very last second. Several of his comrades did not have such luck; I. and III. *Gruppen* both suffered two pilots killed and one wounded, among them *Oblt.* Hans Ehlers who made a wheels-up landing after having shot down a P-51 and a B-17.

If Ehlers was only lightly wounded, the same was not the case, three days later, for his *Gruppenkommandeur*, *Hptm.* Schnoor. An engine failure on a local flight marked the end of his career with JG 1. The supply officer of I. *Gruppe*, *Hptm.* Ludwig Siegfried, recalled: "On Sunday, 16 April 1944, *Hauptmann* Schnoor came to see me to ask if, as usual, lunch would be served at 13.00 hours. I said it would. It was midday. There was an hour for him to do some local flying. No one knew exactly what happened. Schnoor tried a forced landing in a field. The undercarriage could not take the force of the landing and snapped. He was badly injured in the head. Taken to hospital at Detmold, he remained there for six weeks. His marriage had been arranged for this time, and he literally went from his hospital bed to his wedding ceremony."

On 19 April, the Eighth Air Force dealt a serious blow to JG 1. No fewer than 772 bombers under strong escort headed for a variety of targets, most of them *Luftwaffe* installations. Among them was Paderborn, III./JG 1's base. JG 1 took off before the bombs rained down from the 117 B-24s which crossed the airfield. A violent battle with the escort cost the *Geschwader* five killed and one wounded, as well as the loss of *Oblt.* Eder's 'Yellow 4' when he was forced to bale out. There were only three *Abschüsse* (two B-17s claimed by *Flg.* Blech and *Oblt.* von Kirchmayr and a P-51 by *Ogfr.* Peischl). On the ground there was catastrophe; about 20 of III./JG 1's Bf 109s were damaged or destroyed. The landing strip was blasted by more than 184 tons of HE bombs and the resultant craters forced the *Gruppe* to land on a neighbouring field. Nevertheless, quick and vigorous repairs to the damaged installations ensured that those Bf 109s which managed to escape the carnage were back on the field within 24 hours.

On 22 April, 803 bombers once again headed into skies over the Reich, the majority of them towards the marshalling yards at Hamm. Aircraft from all of JG 1's component units took off shortly before 18.00 hrs. III. *Gruppe* came off worst in the ensuing combat with the formidable fighter escort provided by 242 P-51s. Seven pilots of III. *Gruppe* were killed and two wounded. Nevertheless, four pilots (*Hptm.* Eberle, *Hptm.* Grislawski, *Hptm.* Burkhardt and *Ofw.* Kaiser) claimed four Mustangs. Burkhardt had to bale out shortly after his victory and he survived attack from two P-51s while hanging from his parachute. I. and II. *Gruppen* were luckier; a joint attack allowed them to claim five P-47s and eight B-17s. Among the victorious pilots were *Oblt.* Georg Eder, (one P-47), *Ofw.* Otto Bach (one P-47), *Fw.* Walter Köhne (one B-17) and Reinhard Flecks (two P-47s). *Flieger* Georg Blech claimed a 'double' – two B-17s. After having shot down the first bomber from behind, he collided with the rudder of a second whilst breaking off combat with the first. Both aircraft went down but Blech, as well as

seven Americans from the second B-17, managed to bale out. The I. *Gruppe* suffered one pilot killed and two wounded, and II. *Gruppe* one killed and one wounded.

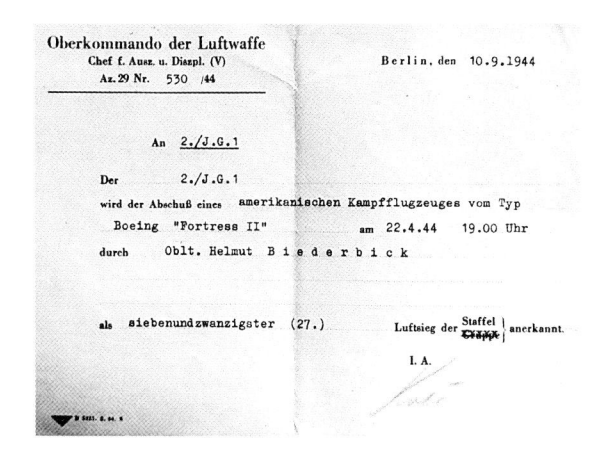

The young *Oberfähnrich* Herbert Neuner recalled his early combat experience at this time: "Born in 1924, I was 18 when I volunteered for service. My aim was to become a pilot. After doing four months of drill, I was posted to the *Luftkriegschule* 4, then to pilot school where I received accelerated training. In August 1943, I was at a fighter training unit, *Jagdgeschwader* 104 at Herzogenaurach. In March 1944, I arrived at Orange where *Jagdgruppe Süd* was located, from where the fighter units in the West drew fresh pilots from the pool of reserves. At this point, every young pilot hoped for the order which gave their posting to the front. Mine soon arrived – I was to join JG 1. My dream had come true with, at first, a stop-over in Paris. After a train journey in the company of *Fähnrich* Gustav Knoll, I arrived at Rheine on 5 April 1944. *Hauptmann* Schnoor received us, and then separated us; I was posted to 2. *Staffel*, Knoll to 3. *Staffel*. We had to learn to fly the Fw 190; neither of us had had it in our hands before. *Oberfeldwebel* Demuth was my tutor, even after my first take-off when I nearly killed myself. Three take-offs in a day and it was felt I was ready. The following day, I was presented to the *Kommodore*, the famous Walter Oesau who received us warmly and left a lasting impression. Shortly after, the *Gruppe* left for Rheine for the combat area of Bad Lippspringe. It was a large field with an imposing building, a boarding house where we pilots were billeted. In the morning a wagon or coach came to collect us and take us to the airfield. Waiting for the 'Alert', we passed the day playing cards, some fished, others listened to records. The most popular type was 'swing'; the discs had been 'liberated' from France and they were listened to with great pleasure, ignoring the ban on this kind of music. My first combat mission unfortunately just petered out: I. *Gruppe* were badly directed, and we returned disappointed. The second was much more eventful. On 22 April, the *Gruppe* was scrambled. The *Stab* took off first, then each *Staffel* in turn, *Schwarm* by *Schwarm*. Like a long ribbon, our formation climbed for sufficient altitude. I was far from being afraid. It was a new, exciting experience. We attacked the *Viermots* head-on. After this pass, our formation was split up, but I managed to join a comrade who appeared to have been hit. After that, I can't remember anything. My aircraft was hit, almost certainly by our own *Flak*. In spite of the danger of explosion, and against the orders of his superiors, a *Feldwebel* from a nearby battery succeeded in getting me out of my burning Fw 190. I was hospitalised until 5 July."

On this day *Major* Heinz Bär recorded his 200th victory shortly before 20.00 hrs, making him the seventh pilot to do so. Bär's victory also represented the 122nd victory for *Stab* II./JG 1 and the 687th for II./JG 1. The pilots were gathered on the runway at Störmede discussing aspects of their last sortie, when they saw a lone B-24 heading west. Bär took off quickly, moved in behind the Liberator and one pass in his Fw 190 A-7 'Red 23', was sufficient to bring it down. Four crew baled out.

On 24 April, the unit recorded five claims against B-17s (including three *Herausschüsse*) and two over P-47s for no losses. There was also a probable claim over a Thunderbolt by *Uffz*. Fritz Haspel of 8. *Staffel*.

On 28 April, 9./JG 1's *Ofw*. Roman Heimbach and *Uffz*. Werner Humer (the latter had been with JG 1 for only four days) were lost under tragic

ABOVE LEFT: For a Luftwaffe fighter pilot to have a claimed victory confirmed it had to be accepted and authorised by an official commission. This often took several months and on many occasions the pilot had been killed in the meantime. This is an example of a confirmation form for a victory claimed on 22 April 1944, received, in this instance, by Oblt. Biederbick who survived the war.

ABOVE: Major Bär (back to camera) and Oblt. Eder (to his right) talk with pilots of 6. Staffel at Störmede, spring 1944. On the left of the group are Oberfeldwebeln Otto Bach and Leo Schuhmacher.

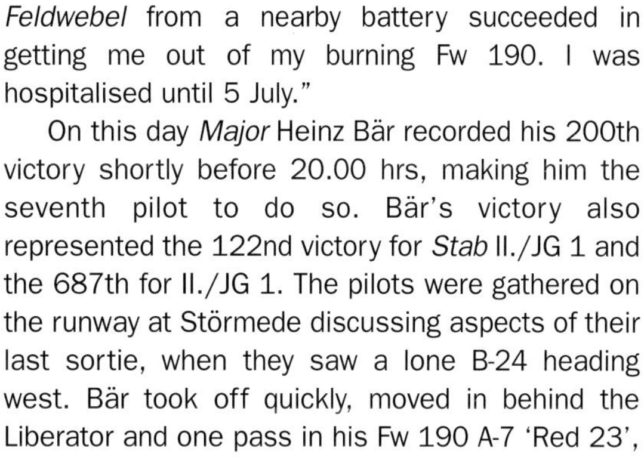

LEFT: Two major fighter commanders and ace – the Kommodore of JG 1, Walter Oesau and Gruppenkommandeur of II./JG 1, Major Heinz Bär – walk side-by-side. The Fieseler Storch in the background was frequently used by them to visit the crash sites of their victims.

LEFT: Oberst Walter Grabmann, the Kommandeur of 3. Jagddivision under whose control JG 1 came, frequently visited his pilots in his Fw 190 A-6 'White X'. He is seen here with Major Heinz Bär (left) and Oberst Walter Oesau (right) at Störmede, April 1944.

RIGHT: Störmede, April 1944. Major Heinz Bär (centre in profile) converses with Oblt. Georg Peter Eder, Staffelkapitän of 6./JG 1. To the right is Ofw. Leo Schuhmacher (Bär's wingman).

ABOVE AND RIGHT: Fw. Alfred Bindseil of 6./JG 1 returns from a mission in his Fw 190 A-8 'Yellow 11', Spring 1944.

circumstances. Their *Staffelkapitän*, *Oblt.* Erich Buchholz had assigned them and their Bf 109s for a simulated air combat with his younger brother *Lt.* Günther Buchholz of 6./JG 1 who was to fly a Fw 190. Having avoided the approach of the Bf 109s, *Lt.* Buchholz went into a dive and straightened at only four or five metres (13-16 ft) from the ground. Both pursuers crashed and were killed.

On 29 April, the complete *Geschwader*, including 27 Fw 190s of II. *Gruppe*, took off shortly before 10.00 hrs to intercept a bomber armada heading to Berlin. I. and II. *Gruppen* again claimed several victories; four P-47s, eight B-17s (including two *Herausschüsse*) and a B-24. The latter was downed by *Major* Bär who had also shot down a P-47. Other victorious pilots were *Oblt.* Eder (one P-47 and 1 B-17 in Fw 190 A-8 'Yellow 4'), *Oblt.* von Kirchmayr (one P-47 in Fw 190 A-7 'Black 1'), as well as two aces from I./JG 1, *Ofw.* Piffer and *Ofw.* Hübl.

Heinz Bär reported: "On 29 April 1944, I was at cockpit readiness in my 'Red 13'. I took off with the Gruppe at 09.40 hours. In concert with I. and III. Gruppe, we headed in the direction of Kassel, via Paderborn, and reached 7,000 metres. On a course of 130 degrees in the Hannover region we saw the enemy formation made up of Boeings and Liberators with a strong fighter escort. They were heading due east. We gained height and opened our attack near Braunschweig. After I had shot down a Liberator, our formation, assailed by the fighter escort, entered into a merciless combat. I tried to regain height in a sharp climb. At this moment, above me, I spotted a Fw 190 with its right undercarriage leg hanging down. It was being chased by a Thunderbolt. I got directly behind the latter and opened fire at a distance of 150 metres. The P-47 exploded. Its debris was scattered to the south of Braunschweig. It was 10.56 hours. Height 7,500 m. Witness: Ofw. Schuhmacher."

When the battle was over, six pilots from I. and II./JG 1 landed at Salzwedel. After a brief rest, *Oblt.* von Kirchmayr took off at the head of a *Schwarm* to catch the bombers on the return flight. Five more victories were claimed at about 13.15 hrs, among them a B-24 and a B-17 for Kirchmayr who recorded the 700th victory of II. *Gruppe*, the 195th of 5.*Staffel* and his own fifteenth *Abschüss*. The 6./JG 1 lost two pilots: *Ogfr.* Werner Triebel and *Uffz.* Hans-Hasso Homfeld.

For the time being, the main task of the Allied air forces was the preparation for the planned invasion of Europe. The German communications network had to be destroyed, or at least seriously disrupted. Although Allied superiority was overwhelming, *Luftwaffe* units operating in the *Reichsverteidigung,* or 'Defence of the Reich', and on the Western Front were being reinforced. Profiting from a relative calm in the east, the *Luftwaffe* was able to amass some 1,675 aircraft in Germany and the West. All the units based in

ABOVE: *22 April 1944 was a notable day for Major Bär; shortly after landing from a combat mission, the Kommandeur took off once again at 19:53 hrs after having sighted a lone B-24 flying over Störmede. He returned 27 minutes later with his 200th victory. These views show him following his victorious return.*

LEFT: *Lt. Günther Buchholz of 6./JG 1.*

RIGHT: The three Buchholz brothers, all of them pilots, two of whom served with II./JG 1: Lt Günther Buchholz (left), killed on 31 May 1944 with 6./JG 1 and Oblt Erich Buchholz (centre) who lost his life after the war when he crashed in a civilian aircraft in Ireland in 1961. To the right is Hans Buchholz who was killed in action in Russia whilst serving as a Stuka pilot

the West however, were exhausted from their continuous battles with the Allied fighter escorts. The first half of 1944 was a murderous time for the day fighters; between January and May, nearly 1,850 fighter pilots had been killed. Each unit was frequently weakened by the loss of experienced officers. For example, JG 2 lost two *Kommodore* (*Obstlt.* Mayer and *Major* Ubben) in less than two months. These types of experienced pilots would be sorely missed when the Allied invasion came.

An order was issued to German pilots to evade combat with the escort fighters. The bombers remained the primary objective. From then on, the Allied fighters, whose range by now allowed them to reach just about every corner of the Reich, could fly almost with impunity. Their numbers and their quality contributed to their forming a screen for the bombers which became harder and harder to penetrate.

On 8 May, Berlin and Braunschweig were the targets for 807 bombers escorted by 729 fighters. Towards 08.40 hrs, the three *Gruppen* took off and assembled over Paderborn. Four B-24s and 1 B-17 were claimed by II. *Gruppe*, the familiar names of Eder, von Kirchmayr and Schuhmacher among the claimants. With seven claims, I. *Gruppe* was also successful, *Uffz.* Kurt Geberth of 1. *Staffel* shooting down a B-24 and recording a *Herausschuss* over another. *Lt.* Piffer, recently promoted to officer rank and *Staffelkapitän* of 1./JG 1, was victorious over a P-51 and *Ofw.* Hübl, a B-17. But neither Geberth nor Hübl would profit from their victories, the former being killed a few seconds later, the latter being severely wounded. They were not the only casualties from I. *Gruppe*; three other pilots were killed and *Uffz.* Wilhelm

One of the last photos of Oberst Walter Oesau during a visit to his I. Gruppe. Oesau is seen here with Oblt. Hans Ehlers (right).

Peine had to join Hübl in hospital. The day would also see what was to be the 118th and last victory for the *Kommodore*, Walter Oesau, when he downed a P-47.

At 11.42 hrs, *Oblt.* Rüdiger von Kirchmayr once again took off with his wingman and shot down another B-17. His companion, *Flieger* Georg Blech, shot down a P-51 over Cloppenburg. In the meantime, III./JG 1 claimed its only victory on that day when a P-51 was brought down by *Oblt.* Erich Buchholz. But the *Gruppe* lost three pilots killed and one wounded.

11 May 1944 was a black day for *Jagdgeschwader* 1. The Eighth Air Force carried out its 350th bombing mission since its first raid in mid-August 1942, with attacks on marshalling yards in north-eastern France, Belgium and Luxembourg. Nearly 900 bombers took part, and the fighter escort flew over 1,000 sorties. At Paderborn, the Bf 109 Gs of *Stab* and III. *Gruppe* took off in the afternoon, *Kommodore* Walter Oesau leading off three aircraft of the *Stabsschwarm*. They were followed by the Bf 109 G-6s and G-6 ASs of III./JG 1, led by *Major* Hartmann Grasser. Oesau, with 125 victories to his credit, was taking off on what was to prove his final mission. The four machines of the *Stabsschwarm* were diving towards the bombers when they were pounced on by a horde of American fighters. Oesau was forced into a circling combat, alone against five enemy aircraft. His wingmen, themselves fully occupied by the action, could do nothing to help him. Trying to escape his opponents and defend himself, Oesau

progressively lost height. *Ofw.* Leo Schuhmacher recalled: "Several times I had said to Oesau that the Fw 190 was better than the Bf 109, but being an old 109 pilot, he preferred it. On 11 May, Bär remained on the ground because of technical problems and Oesau led the formation totalling 30 aircraft. At high altitude we spotted the enemy fighters and Oesau ordered me over the radio to take II. *Gruppe* with me. As I was later told by his wingman, a young *Oberfähnrich*, Oesau was attacked by P-51s which forced him into a turning dogfight. Each turn became tighter, and the Bf 109 slowed down, more so than his adversaries. Oesau was probably shot down near the ground. I saw Oesau's body; the whole left side of him appeared to have been hit by a burst. Thus wounded, he no doubt tried to carry out a makeshift landing."

The remains of his Bf 109 G-6 AS, 'Green 13' were found several kilometres from St. Vith in Belgium. His body was found not far away. It had been flung clear on impact. *Major* Bär had the sad task of identifying it. Several years after the war, *Major* Hartmann Grasser, an *Eichenlaubträger* with close on 100 victories gained in both the East and West and who had just taken over III./JG 1 from *Hptm.* Friedrich Eberle, also commented on Oesau's loss: "At that time, Oesau was physically and mentally exhausted. Many German fighter pilots had to fight right through the war, without respite. I consider it a grave error on the part of our High Command. I personally took part in the combat when Oesau was lost. Alone, chased by Lightnings and Mustangs, he had no chance of escaping. Neither did we. It was in this way that we lost the majority of the best among us."

A local civilian also remembered Oesau's death: "On 11 May 1944, I was playing with my brother and both my sisters on our farm, 'La Merlé', when we heard the sound of a tremendous air battle above us. My mother was frightened and ran into the cellar with my sisters, while I and my brother remained upstairs to watch the battle. My mother was very anxious because my father was working in the field right under the fighting. We heard an aircraft crash. Later, my father told me that the Messerschmitt hit the ground, rebounded and came down again without exploding. He found the pilot dead. Several shell cases and pieces of equipment were lying on the ground around the destroyed aircraft. German soldiers were not long in arriving. My father was told that this was a highly-decorated officer. Because they were unable to reach the scene of the crash (1 km north-west of the small town of Beho) with their vehicle, they requisitioned my father and his cart. They laid the badly injured body on the cart and my father pushed it to the chapel of the 'Château de la Concession' where they laid the body to rest.

"Of course, we spoke much about this crash and of the pilot and so we learned that it was a top ace named Oesau. When my father took me to the chapel two days later to see the body, it had already been removed, but a large blood stain was still there. We heard that another officer of the same unit, a man called Hartmann Grasser, was very angry when he heard that his officer had been carried in a cart by a farmer. This seemed to have been a major disgrace."

Much research has been carried out to establish Oesau's assailant. Nothing certain has been resolved. One theory is that his canopy was hit during the attack on the bombers by a shell fired by the American, Colonel James L. 'Pappy' Doyle. Oesau tried to break off combat, and was followed by five P-38s, holding his own against them for ten minutes, before trying to land as a matter of urgency and being shot down as a result. In a sad twist of fate, several hours after Oesau's disappearance, a letter signed by Adolf Galland, the *General der Jagdflieger*, arrived at the unit's *Stab*. It was an order posting Oesau to Galland's headquarters staff. But by then it was too late. All that could be done was to honour the fallen hero. From henceforth, the premier fighter unit would be known as '*Jagdgeschwader* 1 *Oesau*'. *Major* Heinz Bär, the most experienced pilot in the unit, was immediately considered to be the new *Kommodore*. But having recently been appointed *Kommodore* of JG 3, he remained with JG 1 for only another ten days before moving to this new unit. *Oblt.* Georg Eder became *Gruppenführer* of II. *Gruppe* in the interim.

The Eighth Air Force gave the *Luftwaffe* no respite. On 12 May, it launched a major raid against the oil industries of eastern Germany. The three *Gruppen* of JG 1 took off and assembled over Paderborn at around 11.00 hrs. As usual, III. *Gruppe* was the first to become involved with the escort fighters. The *Gruppe* lost one pilot killed, *Fw.* Hans-Joachim Gebser of 7. *Staffel*, and at least three aircraft for no successes. But the

As with his predecessor, Oberst Walter Oesau, Kommodore of JG 1 was afforded a full military funeral procession.

Three pilots from II./JG 1 enjoy a laugh at Störmede, May 1944. From left to right: Oblt. Schüller, Fw. Brunner and Ofw. Schuhmacher.

RIGHT: One famous fighter pilot replaced another: Obstlt. Herbert 'Ihle' Ihlefeld, the ninth member of the Wehrmacht to receive the Schwerten (swords) to the Ritterkreuz (Oesau had been the third; Bär, the seventh and Philipp, the eighth) left JG 11 and became Kommodore of JG 1 at the end of May 1944. He would led the unit until the war's end. He died in July 1995.

ensuing battle was even costlier for II./JG 1; five pilots were killed, including the promising *Uffz.* Helmut Stiegler. However, the balance was somewhat redressed by a victory over a P-47 and five B-24s (including three *Herausschüsse*).

On 13 May, things looked better for III./JG 1. While all three *Gruppen* grappled with the US escort, III. *Gruppe* emerged as the most successful with four P-47s claimed by two 7./JG 1 pilots, *Ofw.* Kaiser and *Uffz.* Greber and two pilots from the *Gruppenstab*, *Lt.* Koplik and *Ofw.* Timm. In I./JG 1, *Lt.* Piffer survived a wheels-up landing unhurt after having been rammed by a P-47. Less fortunate, the American pilot crashed into the sea. A Mustang pilot experienced a similar fate when his rudder was damaged by *Fw.* Bindseil's (6./JG 1) propeller, just before being riddled by the German's guns. The new *Kommandeur*, Hartmann Grasser, was assured of his fighter-pilots' abilities; his many meetings, briefings and 'bawling-outs' finally paid off.

Six days later, on 19 May, towards midday, the unit gathered over Paderborn to face another raid on Berlin. The escort managed to prevent the first head-on attack. Two P-47s were claimed by *Ofhr.* Swoboda and *Ofw.* Schuhmacher. The Germans turned east before launching a second frontal attack ten minutes later. *Oblt.* 'Schorsch' Eder added to his success with a B-24 and two P-47s. Two further P-47s as well as seven B-24s (including five *Herausschüsse*) were claimed by pilots of I. and II. *Gruppen*. Nevertheless, these successes cost JG 1 four pilots killed and one wounded.

Walter Oesau's successor was another top quality fighter pilot. Like those who had preceded him (Philipp, Oesau and Bär), he had received one of the German forces' highest awards: the *Ritterkreuz* with Oakleaves and Swords. Officially named *Kommodore* of JG 1 on 20 May 1944, with over 1,000 combat missions since the Spanish Civil War, close on 130 victories, including 15 *Viermots*, *Oberstleutnant* Herbert Ihlefeld had considerable combat and command experience. JG 1 was the fifth unit he had led.

On 24 May, *Jagdgeschwader* 1's strength was as follows:

Stab	Bad Lippspringe	no aircraft on strength
I. Gruppe	Bad Lippspringe	28 (11 serviceable)
II. Gruppe	Störmede	27 (16)
III. Gruppe	Paderborn	48 (21)

On that day, the American 2nd Bomb Division sent its B-24s to prepare for the Invasion, targeting several airfields in France. Meanwhile, the 1st and 3rd Bomb Divisions paid a visit to Berlin. JG 1 and JG 3 approached the armada together. Because of intense *Flak*, a mass assault *Gruppe* could not be formed. Attacks were therefore made in pairs or in *Schwarm* formation. One B-17 each was claimed by *Lt.* Bach in Fw 190 A-7, 'White 2' and *Oblt.* von Kirchmayr, the latter's claim, however, not confirmed. 1. *Staffel*, claimed three B-17s while 8./JG 1 reported the destruction of a B-17 accredited to *Lt.* Koplik, a P-38 to *Gefr.* Penke and a P-51 to *Ofw.* Timm without loss.

The next day, as *Lt.* Franz Koplik recorded a further success, young *Ofhr.* Hubert Heckmann met the enemy for the first time: "On 25 May 1944, I took part in my second combat flight. I overslept that morning, arrived too late at the bus stop and therefore had to walk the five kilometres from Kirchborchen to our dispersal. At dispersal we were on *Sitzbereitschaft*. I grabbed two slices of bread from the breakfast table, and our orderly, Meier, placed a fried egg between them, while I fastened my seat belts. After assembly, we flew south. I was No. 4 in our flight and additionally the Y-pilot.

"Often the Y-device was placed in a rookie's aircraft. The device broadcast a frequency that allowed a bearing from the ground. The frequency was changed daily. It was my duty to tune it every morning. Therefore I had my first take-off at an unearthly hour. The ground station informed us all along the way about our position. The disadvantage for the Y-pilot was that although he was able to listen to all calls and he was also able to communicate with the ground stations, he wasn't able to communicate with his flight comrades. Our *Gruppe* consisted of about 20 aircraft, with 9. *Staffel* with two *Schwärme* in the air. Our *Schwarm*, consisting of *Lt.* Koplik, *Uffz.* Helmut Fröhlich, *Fw.* Walter Pleines and me, flew at the back of the formation. After some time, we saw the Alps in the distance, and in front of it a blanket of smog, maybe München. Our altitude was about 8,000 metres in a clear mid-summer sky. Around 09.00, the ground station ordered us to turn around and land at Herzogenaurach. After the turn, Franz Koplik let the distance between our *Schwarm* and the rest of the formation continuously grow. The formation descended, but Koplik continued on the former altitude. After some time, the ground station ordered us to circle; we were handed over to another air control region. While doing a circle we would normally have to wait several minutes before the overtaking air control region informed us about our actual position. Sometimes it happened that they used a 180 degree different bearing, so that they would have placed us far to the north in such a case.

"Normally, this total procedure took about five minutes, but this time we heard the incoming call after just a few seconds. The new control ordered us, without naming our position, not to land in Herzogenaurach, but to land in Frankfurt. The pronunciation 'Fränkford' made me prick up my ears. I answered: '*Rikardo*!' (which means effectively '*I haven't understood*!'). The repeat followed immediately with an almost annoyed voice: '*Do not land in Herzogenaurach, land in Fränkford, the area is clear of the enemy.*' Now I noticed that the 'r' had a very strong accent, like I had learned in school during English lessons. I tuned my transmitter to the formation frequency and warned my fellow pilots: '*Attention! Counterfeiter!*' (the code for foreign agents). I'd just finished my warning when my flight mates overflew me. A bunch of Mustangs was advancing from below. Everything happened so fast that I wasn't able to react and simply flew straight ahead. Thus I was sitting around uselessly.

"I had no choice but to keep to the regulations and went over to low-level flight at once. At this altitude it was very dusty. I saw neither my comrades nor the Mustangs. During my descent, I heard Franz Koplik with his Viennese accent: '*Hob oahn obigschossen!*' (which means 'I downed one!'). In front of me, I saw a mushroom cloud rising from the ground and a single wing drop down like a faded leaf. I did a 360 above this position to show Franz that I had witnessed the 'hit, so he had a witness for his report. I levelled off, but recognised from the position of the sun, that I was flying westwards in the direction of France. I just turned to a northerly heading when I saw at my 10 o'clock position a plane far away heading north at the same altitude. Assuming that it was a poor sod like me, I folded down the Revi (reflex visor) and switched off the weapons. Meanwhile – looking outside in all directions – we came so close that I was able to identify the type of plane; it was a P-51 Mustang with a black cowling! I had just enough time to switch on the weapons again and to pull down the trigger to 'fire'. I had to aim with my tracer bullets, and the bullets whizzed above his fuselage.

"In a dog curve, I climbed up 10 metres and had meanwhile brought the Revi into position. He flew just a little below me and I was able to see his head from behind. Because he flew straight ahead and made no attempt to break and to take me on, I shut my left eye. Again, the rounds whizzed close above his fuselage. My 2 cm MG jammed. Only three to five bullets left the MG, and then another jam. I loaded through, fired another bullet, and then all three guns were jammed. Meanwhile I had approached to within three to five metres and said to myself: '*When I turn away from him now, he'll fire at me, but he's going to go down anyway.*' Therefore my only chance was the ram push. My intention was to get the Iron Cross First Class. They said that a pilot got one point for the downing of a single engine aircraft by gunfire and three times as much for downing it by ramming. And it needed three points to get the Iron Cross First Class.

"It was clear to me that I had to come in from behind and smash his tail unit. My only worry was that I could lose my engine. We were 50 metres above the ground, not nearly enough to exit the aircraft with my parachute. In front of us I saw the village of Botenheim. I planned to pass it and ram the Mustang behind the village because if the Mustang went down in the village it could cause damage. Just in front of the village, my enemy banked slightly to the left and pulled up. I expected that he would begin to defend himself. I had no idea how our aircraft would react when the ram happened in razor flight. I pushed to get out of his propeller wash and gave full throttle. When I was just one metre away from him, I pulled up. I heard the bang when hitting him and pushed down again. Now I only heard the airstream which was intensified by the Mustang's tail unit on my cowling. I looked out for a suitable landing area close to one of the villages, so that I would not be too far from a telephone. I had to underfly a high tension line and jumped out of the aircraft immediately after it came to a stop. Because I heard suspicious noises from the front of my aircraft I ran away, thinking that the cause was a fire. But the hissing noise came from escaping coolant. The cooler was broken as a result of my crash landing, and a little cloud of steam rose up into the air.

"With a rude tone, I got orders to return to Paderborn by train. After my return, my *Kommandeur*, *Major* Grasser, told me that he ordered me to ride by train because he thought that I rammed the Mustang through my own stupidity. Then he put the Iron Cross Second Class in my hand, about which I was really disappointed."

On 28 May, JG 1's three *Gruppen* took off at 13.05 hrs and assembled over Paderborn led by *Oblt*. Kirchmayr. They would enjoy considerable success with 23 victories including 12 *Herausschüsse*. I. *Gruppe* returned an impressive score, claiming 15 B-17s. In *Stab*/III. *Gruppe*, *Lt*. Halbey recorded his second victory over a P-51. However, losses were high; four wounded and three killed, including the experienced *Ofw*. Fritz Timm in Bf 109 G-6, 'Yellow 3'. Timm had moved from I. *Gruppe* to III. *Gruppe* when the latter *Gruppe* was formed. One of III./JG 1's wounded pilots, *Gefr*. Josef Körner, was declared unfit for further flying. He was the cousin of the *Ritterkreuzträger*, Friedrich Körner, the legendary ace, Hans-Jochen Marseille's close friend.

Ofhr. Hubert Heckmann of 9./JG 1 recalled: "Really early in the morning, *Hptm*. Burkhardt, *Lt*. Hans Halbey, *Fw*. Fritz Timm and myself were ordered to cockpit readiness via loudspeaker. It was planned to get us to go after enemy formations returning from a raid. I took a reserve machine, took my parachute to it, but I couldn't find my flying helmet, which I had probably left the day before in my quarters. Before I was able to find a suitable helmet, the other three took off. They came across a formation of 30 Mustangs. Hans Halbey later came to me and told me what had happened; Burkhardt was able to get out of trouble because of his excellent flying skills. Halbey's cabin was smashed and he was injured by shattered glass. Fortunately his eyes were OK. After that, he jumped from his aircraft by parachute. Fritz Timm held on very well for a while, but then got into bad trouble. The last words heard by Halbey were: '*Help me – I can't stand it any more.*' Then he crashed and was killed. Fritz Timm was most respected in our group because of his exemplary behaviour and his balanced character. This mission would have certainly been the third and last for me. Halbey congratulated me because I hadn't participated in it."

On 29 May, from 08.15 hrs, the German listening service monitored bombers forming up over Ipswich. At 11.01 hrs after waiting for 15 minutes in their aircraft, 20 pilots of II./JG 1 took off towards Paderborn. There they formed up with the other two *Gruppen* of the unit at 1,000 m. At midday, the unit located the enemy and flew parallel to the formation for several minutes. III./JG 1, as usual, had the hard task of taking on the escort. *Hptm*. Burkhardt claimed a P-47. Meanwhile, I. and II./JG 1 increased speed, overtook the bombers and turned in for a frontal attack. *Oblt*. Eder, *Lt*. Bach and *Lt*. Swoboda, as well as two comrades from II. *Gruppe* shot down five B-17s. II. *Gruppe* also claimed four *Herausschüsse*. Short of fuel, 13 Fw 190s landed at Cottbus. One pilot was killed on landing, while Eder and Bach were wounded.

At the end of Spring 1944, OKL decided to reinforce all fighter units based in the West. A fourth *Staffel* was considered necessary once the Allies launched the Invasion.

I./JG 1 was supplemented by 9./JG 77 under *Oblt*. Wolfgang Ernst, a veteran of that unit since 1941. Recently wounded in combat over Rumania, he left convalescence to take up his new posting at an airfield near Uelzen where his pilots were to be trained on the Fw 190 A-8, JG 77 having flown only the Bf 109. The conversion was completed in three days.

The 7./JG 51 was assigned to II./JG 1. The order to transfer reached the unit at Terestopol near Brest-Litowsk where the front was relatively stable. The *Staffelkapitän* was *Ritterkreuzträger*, *Hptm*. Karl-Heinz Weber with 136 victories in the east to his credit. Pilots started arriving at II./JG 1's airfield at Störmede on 29 May. Here they had to convert from the Bf 109 to the Fw 190. This transition passed without any major problems as the *Staffel* had previously flown the Fw 190. They had just arrived when a somewhat surprising came in; *Hptm*. Weber was to leave the *Staffel* to take over III./JG 1. The Austrian, *Lt*. Friedrich Krakowitzer (nicknamed 'Kraksel'), would become '*Staffelführer*' of 7./JG 51.

III. *Gruppe* were provided with bomber pilots who had converted to fighters, a move which became more prevalent as losses mounted in the *Jagdwaffe*. These excellent pilots often did not have the experience or qualities required of fighter pilots and as such, they were converted to a role which was unfamiliar to them. The 1./KG 2 released 62 *Unteroffiziere* and ground personnel to III./JG 1, becoming effective from mid-October. Another change at the head of the *Gruppe* saw *Major* Hartmann Grasser hand his command to *Hptm*. Karl-Heinz Weber.

These three reinforcement *Staffeln* were re-named 4., 8. and 12. *Staffeln* from 15 July. These changes did not take effect until September. The men would have other matters to occupy their minds.

Berlin Debut **239**

Focke-Wulf Fw 190 'White 3'
1./JG 1
March 1944

LEFT: *Fw 190 'White 3' of 1./JG 1 on the perimeter track.*

BELOW: *Fw 190 A 'Red 22' of Stab II./JG 1 at Störmede, April 1944 – a machine probably flown by Ofw. Leo Schuhmacher.*

BELOW: *The usual mount of Ofw. Leo Schuhmacher was Fw 190 A-7 'Red 23'. Major Bär recorded his 200th victory in this machine.*

Focke-Wulf Fw 190 A-7 'Red 13'
Major Heinz Bär
II./JG 1
Rheine
March 1944

ABOVE: A close-up of the rudder marking on Major Bär's aircraft.

ABOVE AND RIGHT:
Major Heinz Bär's Fw 190 A-7 'Red 13' (W.Nr. 431007) with – in above photograph – its rudder decoration showing 200 victories.

Two views of Oblt. von Kirchmayr's Fw 190 A 'Yellow 13' during the Spring of 1944, piloted here by one of his comrades, Uffz. Milde or Ofw. Haninger. Note the Defence of the Reich red fuselage band as well as the antenna for the FuG 16 ZE radio.

**Focke-Wulf Fw 190 A 'Yellow 13'
Oblt. Rüdiger von Kirchmayr
II./JG 1
possibly at Störmede
March-April 1944**

242 JG 1 – Defenders of the Reich

Fw 190 As of 6./JG 1 at Störmede in April 1944 carrying the Geschwader emblem and 'Defence of the Reich' red fuselage band.

Focke-Wulf A-?
6./JG 1
Störmede
April 1944

Two of the first Fw 190 A-8s delivered to 6./JG 1 at the end of March/beginning of April 1944. Neither aircraft is fitted with outer guns in the wings.

BELOW: On 9 April 1944, following intense combat with American four-engined bombers in deplorable weather, two Fw 190 A-8s of 1./JG 1 ('White 3' [W.Nr.170101] and 'White 14' [W.Nr.170050]) made a wheels-up landing on the small island of Aero. Note here the flame dampers over the machine guns. Repaired, 'White 3' was shot down on 22 April 1944.

ABOVE: A scene on the island of Aero, on 9 April 1944 at around 12.30 hrs. Injured in combat, Lt. Hans-Günther Lück of 1./JG 1 crash-landed his Fw 190 A-8 'White 14' (W.Nr.170050).

BELOW: End of April 1944: experienced pilots of II./JG 1 with an unidentified pilot on the left. From the right: Ofw. Otto Bach of 4./JG 1, (14th victory on 22 April), Oblt. Georg-Peter Eder of Stab II./JG 1 (41st victory on 29 April) and Major Heinz Bär, Kommandeur of II./JG 1 (201st and 202nd victories on 29 April).

Focke-Wulf Fw 190 A-8 'White 9'
4./JG 1
Störmede
April 1944

LEFT: Störmede, April 1944. Two of the first Fw 190 A-8s delivered to 4./JG 1 ('White 9' and 'White 2') with red Defence of the Reich bands clearly visible.

Gathered around Fw 190 A-8 'Yellow 7' of Ofhr. Walter Köhne of 3./JG 1 (which is decorated with Köhne's personal emblem 'Löwe') at Bad Lippspringe, May 1944 is, in the cockpit, 1st Wart Obgfr. Kinski, while standing by the aircraft are, from left to right, Ofhr. Gustav Knoll (KIA 21 November 1944), Fw. Eugen Busch (KIA 27 July 1944) and Gefr. Wolfgang Hartung (KIA 18 April 1945).

LEFT: *On 28 May 1944, Uffz. Erwin Steeb of 6./JG 1 shot down a B-17, claiming his first victory. He was wounded the following day.*

BELOW: *Bf 109 G-6/AS of III./JG 1 at Paderborn, May 1944 with 'White 14' of 7./JG 1 in the foreground. Note the red Defence of the Reich fuselage band carrying a small white vertical bar (indicating an aircraft of III. Gruppe).*

Messerschmitt Bf 109 G-6/A 'White 14'
7./JG 1
Paderborn
May 1944

Chapter Eighteen

"Indescribable chaos …"

The Invasion Front – June-July 1944

On 6 June 1944, the Allies landed in Normandy and though the Germans had known that the Invasion was imminent, there had still been uncertainty about precisely where it would take place. Hundreds of possibilities had been studied by German commanders, but for every possibility a German response had been studied. Once it began however, a series of frantic, reactionary orders were sent out and previously planned troop movements put into effect but with little outcome. As far as the German fighter force was concerned, the General Staff had counted on calling upon 1,000 aircraft to combat the Allied air forces over the Invasion front. The *Jagdwaffe,* along with other *Luftwaffe* aircraft would not only be engaged against the greatest aerial umbrella ever put into the sky, they would also have to operate under frequently erratic and ill-conceived command decisions.

Already by the summer of 1943, the *Wehrmacht* had drawn up a plan to oppose an Allied landing in the West. Under the code name '*Drohende Gefahr West*' ('Immediate Danger West'), this plan was continuously amended, adapted to the prevailing situation and the latest information, and improved – until a directive of 27 February which, having been agreed by the *Reichsmarschall*, was applied in earnest. This directive allowed for the transfer, in one day, of the maximum number of flying units (about 1,000 aircraft) to a range of different airfields within about 100 km (62 mls) from any potential landing area. With no idea where such a landing would take place, many forward airfields were made ready from Brittany to Holland, supplied with fuel and ammunition, personnel accommodation and repair facilities.

In June 1944, the strength of German opposition that could readily be sent to oppose a landing attempt amounted to 19 fighter *Gruppen* drawn from *Luftflotte* 2 and *Luftflotte Reich*. These units would reinforce *Luftflotte* 3 which had been established on the Western Front since 1940 and comprised three *Gruppen* of JG 2, three *Gruppen* of JG 26 (plus their respective *Geschwarderstäbe*) and I./JG 301.

In the early hours of 6 June, 1,000 RAF four-engined bombers attacked German positions in the landing area. This armada was soon followed by B-17s and B-24s of the US Eighth Air Force which dropped 3,000 tons of bombs on the same positions, virtually without encountering any aerial opposition! Having concluded these first operations, 1,300 fighter and fighter-bombers of the Eighth Air Force took to the sky supported by single- and twin-engined fighters from the US Ninth Air Force and the British Second Tactical Air Force.

It was under such conditions, and operating under a ratio of 1:10 at best, that JG 1 was to free the skies of enemy bombers and '*Jabos*' and to support German infantry and tanks fighting against the greatest invasion in history.

At 05.00 hrs on the morning of 6 June, *Stab*, I./JG 1 received a coded message: *Einsatz West - Einsatzort Le Mans; Combat Operations West – Operational Base Le Mans*. Thirty minutes later, *Gruppenkommandeur Hptm*. Ehlers assembled his officers and gave the order to prepare to leave Bad Lippspringe airfield. Several hours later, 31 Fw 190 A-8s took off for Montdidier, a staging point en route. Early the following day, they reached Le Mans. During the late afternoon of 6 June, several Ju 52s belonging to 3./TG 1 carrying I./JG 1's technicians and important equipment, took off from Bad Lippspringe. Arriving in the Coulommiers area 40 km (25 mls) east of Paris shortly before midnight, the formation was intercepted by a British night-fighter. A Ju 52, with 16 members of the ground personnel on board, including *Lt*. Sommer, I./JG 1's Intelligence Officer, was shot down. The other aircraft set down quickly as a matter of urgency. *Hptm*. Ludwig Siegfried, the *Gruppe* Supply Officer, took command of 15 wagons from a supply depot. He did not reach Le Mans until the evening of 9 June. A further two days were needed for the arrival of the rest of the unit's equipment.

On 6 June, II./JG 1 left Störmede for Normandy under the command of *Oblt*. Georg-Peter Eder. *Leutnant* Fritz Wegner of 5. *Staffel* recalls: "*Major* Bär, recently transferred to *Jagdgeschwader* 3,

During the Spring of 1944, Ofw. Leo Schuhmacher (far left) and Oblt. Rüdiger von Kirchmayr (far right) were among II./JG 1's best pilots. Both received the Ritterkreuz during the last weeks of the war. On 6 June 1944, II./JG 1 transferred to France without these two aces; Schuhmacher had been with Heinz Bär at JG 3 for several days and von Kirchmayr was ill. They rejoined their Gruppe at Alençon on 12 June. Between these two pilots can be seen Fw. Karl-Heinz Hauptmann and Oberwerksmeister Wilhelm Dietrich.

alerted us by telephone that the Invasion had begun. He advised us to prepare to move to the front. Our 32 Focke-Wulfs took off from Störmede at 16.25 hours. We had a re-fuelling stop-over at Montdidier. This airfield did not have sufficient re-fuelling vehicles, so we had to stay overnight. On the following day, shortly after take-off, we were advised by radio that Flers, the airfield we were heading for, had been bombed. We therefore had to set course for Le Mans. When we arrived, there was indescribable chaos; the ground was completely covered by the sudden influx of masses of aircraft."

For III. *Gruppe,* the Normandy campaign began at 18.00 hrs on 6 June. Seventeen Bf 109 G-6s carried out a 55 minute transfer flight from Paderborn to Beauvais-Tillé. Before the Invasion, a high-altitude fighter unit had been planned comprising the four *Gruppen* of III./JG 1, I./JG 3, I./JG 5 and II./JG 11, whose rôle it was to take on the American bomber escorts. Placed under the control of *Obstlt.* Herbert Ihlefeld, they usually occupied the same airfield. Nevertheless, III./JG 1 often operated independently.

At Le Mans, 7 June began tragically; groundcrew of I. *Gruppe* arrived totally exhausted during the night and slept in their aircraft. During the early morning, American fighter-bombers attacked the airfield and strafed several Ju 52s. Ten bodies were recovered from the aircraft. Simultaneously, 7./JG 51, destined to join II./JG 1, left their base to the north of Paris. At 600 m (1,970 ft), the last *Schwarm* was bounced by Mustangs. Hit, *Lt.* Johann Brünnler had to leave the formation. Six P-51s pursued him. His colleagues, hampered by additional equipment in their cockpits, formed a defensive circle. They became too occupied in defending themselves, and could do nothing for Brünnler. His body and the wreckage of his Fw 190 A-8 were found near Châteaudun. After extricating themselves from the Mustangs, the pilots set down on a part of the famous Le Mans motor-racing circuit. They made their quarters there.

On the ground, as well as in the air, the epicentre of the battle became Caen. I. and II./JG 1 twice flew escort to fighter-bombers. III. *Gruppe* carried out a mission in the same region.

Ofhr. Hubert Heckmann of 9./JG 1 recalls: "After the beginning of the Invasion our *Gruppe* relocated to Beauvais. Our quarters were in the city in the *école normale* (elementary school). All pilots slept in a huge classroom. In Beauvais, I became wingman to the new *Kommandeur*, the *Ritterkreuzträger, Hptm.* Karl-Heinz Weber. That evening, he visited me and talked with me. He was a pleasant, accessible person. His only experience was from the eastern front, and from time to time he used the words '*pull up during air combat*'. I assumed that he would make use of this method in the West and I warned him about doing so. As his *Kaczmarek* I didn't want to lose my *protégé* on the first mission – that would be a bad omen. But he cast all my well-meant recommendations to the wind on our first mission. Weber had a highly polished aircraft and whereas we looked like grey mice, he differed from the rest of the formation. Besides he had Methanol on board.

"On 7 June, we made an early take-off shortly after 08.00 hrs. There was fine weather with cumulus clouds. About 15 aircraft taxied into take-off position with orders for a *Freie-Jagd* in the area around Caen. We took off and headed to the West at an altitude of about 1,000 metres. Near Compiègne about 30 Mustangs showed up, some 500 metres above us. After passing us, they made a downwards turn. Weber didn't turn in, but pulled up steep into the sky, dragging a Methanol cloud behind him. I yelled *'Turn in!'* but he didn't listen to me. I suddenly saw four Mustangs coming down on me and pulled up in a slight left bank to distract them from Weber. My self-sacrifice was of no use; two Mustangs stayed behind me, the other two went after Weber with their superior speed. I fought with my two opponents for more than 30 minutes. They moved off when eventually, they lost much of their speed. The game ended when *Gefr.* Penke unexpectedly passed by and saw me in trouble. He immediately joined the fight, so that the Mustangs left us there and withdrew into the clouds. That evening we were informed that *Hptm.* Weber was dead."

Hptm. Alfred Grislawki of 8. *Staffel* took over the *Gruppe* for the interim. He recalls: "Recovered from the wound I received at the end of January 1944, whilst I was with I. *Gruppe,* I was appointed *Staffelkapitän* of 8. *Staffel*. Continually under attack, the situation in Normandy was unbearable. After landing from a mission, we hurried to eat our rations and then, half an hour later, we were once again in the air trying to save our skins. I recall we all had stomach trouble. The *Amis* circled above our airfields waiting for easy prey which, of course, we were during take-offs and landings. We watched with helpless rage as the enemy dived on our comrades and inflicted heavy losses. No-one was spared by the Americans, not even a pilot hanging on the end of his parachute. We hardly had any officers left. From day to day, young pilots became *Leutnant*, *Staffelführer*, and then eventually they were shot down. I had the feeling that one day soon I would doubtlessly follow my predecessors on the list of losses."

During the Battle of Normandy and with their airfields under continual surveillance, take-offs and landings became the most critical time for the German fighter pilots. This was well illustrated on 7 June at Beauvais; at around 16.00 hrs, several aircraft of III./JG 1 started out on their fourth mission of the day. *Ofhr.* Hubert Heckmann of

Obolt. Georg-Peter 'Schorsch' Eder led II./JG 1 during the early Normandy campaign. He recorded his 50th victory on 21 June 1944 and was awarded the Ritterkreuz three days later. At the end of the war, his tally stood at 78 victories. He died on 11 March 1986.

Lt. Franz Koplik of 9./JG 1 and (left) his Staffelkapitän, Oblt. Erich Buchholz.

9./JG 1 recalls further: "About 16.00, 9. *Staffel* received the take-off order with the same intention as in the morning. Our flight consisted of *Lt.* Koplik, *Uffz.* Fröhlich, *Ofhr.* Heckmann, *Gefr.* Penke and myself. Right after take-off, as our undercarts were going up, Koplik shouted: '*Thunderbolts at 6 o'clock!*' We had about 20 enemy machines on our backs with all guns blazing. Apparently, they had been flying around nearby waiting until we were into our take-off. That meant they got us at our most vulnerable moment. We all went in different directions with only one thought – *every man for himself!* First Koplik was hit. When exiting the aircraft, his foot became caught in the cockpit, and it took a great effort for him to get free. Penke crashed and was killed. Two Thunderbolts got behind Fröhlich and chased him to Köln. I myself opted to make turns to the right, something at which I had trained endlessly as a test pilot in Paderborn. This seemed to work. Carefully, I tried to gain some altitude. This worked as well. The Thunderbolts were behind me the whole time, but they never managed to get into firing position."

But Heckmann did more than just defend himself; he managed to turn inside one of the three P-47s and it slid into the German pilot's Revi sight. He instantly opened fire. At 16:20 hrs, the American went down. However, Heckmann ended his flight with a hard wheels-up landing. He left the wreckage running and avoiding bullets from American fighters which even now followed him as he made for the cover of a nearby wall. No fewer than 16 American fighters circled over his hiding place, but eventually they left to seek other prey.

Just before being shot down and killed, *Gefr.* Werner Penke also claimed a victory over a P-51. By the evening, the surviving pilots felt numbed by the heavy losses incurred on this, the first day on the Invasion Front.

On 8 June, as the Allied armies maintained their pressure and advanced in virtually all sectors, an extraordinary order arrived at I. and II. *Gruppe.* It came as a result of the surprise discovery of an important bomb dump at Le Mans which was equipped with 250 kg (550 lb) bombs. Someone, somewhere had decided they should be put to good use and so the two *Gruppen* were assigned the role of fighter-bombers. This at a time when some pilots lacked even the rudimentary skills of formation flying!

Leutnant Fritz Wegner of 5./JG 1: "Astonishing, even depressing was the fact that we were to become fighter-bombers. None of us had received such training. Someone from a *Jabo* unit arrived and read a text to us, which was supposed to teach us how to use aircraft with bombs. They were suspended under the fuselage, attached to the connecting point for the auxiliary fuel tank. Under these conditions, reaching Normandy from Le Mans was no easy matter, it was necessary to economise on fuel, and above all, avoid interception. To surprise the enemy, we flew due north, over the coast. We hoped to come at them from behind. The coast could be clearly seen ahead. Trouville and Deauville. Obviously, we had an embarrassing choice of targets, but the anti-aircraft fire from the Allied ships was very intense. The sky was saturated with the black puffs of *Flak*. I attacked a ship, but what could a pathetic 250 kilogram bomb do against such a giant? After the attack, we headed due south at low level to pick up course for Le Mans. Judging by the shouts over the radio, the red lamps on the fuel gauges were lighting up soon afterwards. We finally reached Le Mans. I seem to recall that two of our pilots did not return from this attack."

For both I. and II./JG 1, the results of this attack were insignificant. Two other such missions were carried out during the late afternoon of 9 June without incident by 10 and 12 Fw 190s of II. *Gruppe.* Results were no more successful than those of the previous day.

At 01.00 hrs on 10 June, 109 RAF Lancasters and Halifaxes led by Pathfinder Mosquitos bombed the airfield at Le Mans. "During the evening of 9 June," recalls *Hptm.* Ludwig Siegfried, *Oberzahlmeister*, I./JG 1, "we joined our pilots based at Le Mans. I immediately camouflaged the vehicles in a wood. That proved to be sensible, as shortly afterwards at around 01.00 hours, the airfield was the subject of a serious attack. On the airfield and its surroundings, about 50 per cent of our Focke-Wulfs were either destroyed or badly damaged. Those which escaped were grounded. There was no chance of taking off from the badly cratered field. All through the night we were busy, seeking out the unexploded bombs, or watching for another raid. We spent the following hours with shovels and pick-axes making the airfield serviceable – we counted more than 300 craters.

Hptm. Hans Ehlers received the Ritterkreuz on 9 June 1944. He celebrated the occasion with ground personnel from I./JG 1 including the three Spiess (adjutants), recognisable by the double white bands on their sleeves. They were Hptfw. Köditz (1./JG 1), Schnabel (2./JG 1) and Werth (3./JG 1).

After becoming serviceable again, I. *Gruppe* was finally able to take off for the airfield at Cuissai, several kilometres to the north-west of Alençon. But it was an airfield in name only. It consisted of two large fields joined one to the other by a small road. On 12 June, after a lot of work, this 'base' was operational. Such were our valiant preparations for combating the Invasion."

On 12 June, I./JG 1's 12 surviving Fw 190 A-8s took off to embark on two separate patrols. However, progressively brought up to strength, the unit was able to boast 32 Fw 190s twelve days later.

The Fw 190s of II. *Gruppe* dispersed 500 m (1,640 ft) east of the aerodrome were spared. Nevertheless the pilots were unable to take off due to the state of the airfield. Shortly after, II. *Gruppe* took possession of a small improvised airstrip on the edge of the village of Essay, situated ten kilometres from Cuissai/Lonrai.

Fritz Wegner remembered: "The situation for our II. *Gruppe* during combat on the Invasion front was desperate. I know it was the same for the neighbouring units. When we landed, after making those senseless *Jabo* attacks, there were nearly always enemy aircraft circling over the airfield. That was when we had to run like rabbits. For several days, we only ate tinned meat, like tinned beef – morning, midday and evening. Occasionally, our cook would be able to bring us eggs. He would place them carefully in what served as a kitchen. During the night, the Americans would come to bomb us as though they were helping us to make omelettes! After they left, the airfield was no more than a cratered field with unexploded bombs strewn around it. They could explode at any time. The following day, we discovered that one of them had singled out the kitchen! We could see, just to one side, a plate of intact eggs. There followed a serious discussion about being hungry. Suddenly Swoboda and I sprinted to grab the plate. We returned to the cheers of our comrades."

On 11 June, as the Americans were battering Carentan and the British took Tilly-sur-Seulles, the 2nd Bomb Division despatched 584 B-24s to a number of French airfields. Beauvais-Tillé was attacked by 12 Liberators, dropping 30 tons of bombs. The unit's HQ was destroyed, as well as numerous III. *Gruppe* aircraft, which then progressively relocated its pilots to Wunstorf in order to re-equip. In ten days the unit had lost six

Following the loss of many of its aircraft as a result of a raid on its base at Beauvais on 11 June 1944, III./JG 1 returned to Wunstorf to re-equip. Generalleutnant Galland, the General der Jagdflieger (centre of the group facing camera), visited the unit there.

RIGHT: Few pilots from III./JG 1 remained in France following the units return to Wunstorf. However, Ofw. Gustav Dilling (9./JG 1) and Uffz. Ferdinand von Nickisch-Rosenegk (8./JG 1) did, the latter seen here in his Bf 109. Both were killed on 14 June 1944.

Hptm. Erich Woitke presents his men to Generalleutnant Galland, the General der Jagdflieger, at Wunstorf, early July 1944. Most of these men would be lost in action over the Invasion Front.

men, including the experienced *Ofw.* Gustav Dilling shot down near Caen on 14 June. The revitalised *Gruppe* did not reappear over the front until July. By contrast, the *Geschwaderstab* remained in France, albeit without aircraft. On 15 June, it was to be found at Clastres, near St. Quentin.

At Wunstorf, there was a hive of activity; new pilots were made to feel welcome, new Bf 109 G-6s – including many G-6/ASs – were taken on strength and last but not least, the new *Gruppenkommandeur*, 32 year-old *Hptm.* Erich Woitke, an athlete, 1.85 m (6 ft 1 in) tall, who had taken part in the 1936 Olympic decathlon, arrived. He had been with the *Luftwaffe* since 1935, having been a member of the *Legion Condor* (where his four victories made him a well known pilot). Appointed *Staffelkapitän* of 6./JG 3 in February 1940, he became *Hauptmann* and *Kommandeur* of II./JG 52 six months later before moving to several other *Geschwadern* (ZG 1, JG 27, JG 77, JG 11 and JG 300). He enjoyed an excellent reputation amongst his pilots, but not among the various HQ staffs. Woitke was reprimanded and warned several times about his outspokenness. It is said that on one occasion, after having received the *Deutsches Kreuz* in Gold personally from Göring, he threw it to the ground and made disparaging remarks. But in combat, his courage and experience resulted in his steady service advancement.

In Normandy, German fighters continued to be hunted out by the Allies. For that reason, the *Jagdwaffe* operated usually in small numbers on *freie-Jagd* – 'free-hunt' – missions. At 19.00 hrs on 13 June, eight Fw 190s from I./JG 1 were in action in the St. Lô-Ste. Mère Eglise area. *Lt.* Siegfried Stoffel and *Uffz.* Walter Dobrath, both of 1. *Staffel*, recorded I. *Gruppe*'s first victories of the campaign; two Thunderbolts. The two sorties of 14 June were uneventful, but those of the following day near Ste. Mère Eglise and Carentan brought four victories to four of the most effective pilots of that month; an Auster for *Lt.* Anton-Rudolf Piffer and three Thunderbolts for *Lt.* Siegfried Stoffel, *Uffz.* Fritz Rathofer and *Uffz.* Walter Dobrath. However two pilots of III. *Gruppe* were killed; *Uffz.* Ferdinand von Nickisch and the experienced *Ofw.* Gustav Dilling. On the 15th, two pilots of I./JG 1 lost their lives.

On 16 June, poor weather restricted Allied bomber operations, but six Spitfires were credited to I. *Gruppe* following combat over a German column in the Valognes sector. *Lt.* Piffer shot two down, with Stoffel, Rathofer and Dobrath victorious again.

During the combat, *Uffz.* Fritz Hofmann of 3. *Staffel* shot down a Spitfire, but had to bale out at a height of 150 m (492 ft). Wounded and taken to hospital, he was posted missing owing to the poor state of communications at the time. He did not return to the unit until October. The letter sent to his parents by *Staffelkapitän Hptm.* Horst Maier ten Doornkaat describes the action:

"In the region of Caen-Tilly, known for its violent combat, my unit was attacked at about 300 metres by six Spitfires with superior height. All the enemy aircraft were shot down, but they managed to shoot down two of ours. The pilots saw one bale out. The parachute opened, and we overflew where your son landed. We hope that he survived. In spite of intensive checks, we still do not have news of Fritz, which has obliged me to report him as missing. The possibility remains that having been saved by his parachute, he is presently in hospital, and communication difficulties prevent us from knowing more..."

The following day, Fritz Rathofer claimed a 'probable' Mustang, but it was also to be the end of the road for the young Austrian, Anton-Rudolf Piffer. Thunderbolts caught him unawares in his

Fw 190 A-8 'White 3' near Argentan. 'Toni' Piffer was posthumously awarded the *Ritterkreuz* on 20 October 1944 for his 26 victories in the West. Among his victories were 20 four-engined bombers as well as three aircraft claimed during the Normandy campaign.

Hptm. Ludwig Siegfried, *Oberzahlmeister* of I. Gruppe: "Our *Gruppenkommandeur*, *Hauptmann* Hans Ehlers, was really exceptional. Always leading his men, he cared for them individually, in the sky as well as on the ground. One day our clerk told me that he had seen bizarre signals from a neighbouring hill through his binoculars. The following day, our *Gruppenkommandeur* assembled about 20 volunteers and set out to see what it was about. They found no-one, only branches set out in such a way as to be able to guide aircraft, as well as evidence of several impacts on the ground. Obviously, supplies had been dropped for partisans, and this only a short distance from our base. The fact was quickly confirmed, for two or three days later we were fired upon by machine guns from an apparently harmless car. The bullets sprayed everywhere, but no one was wounded. Likewise, our precious radio-wagons parked nearby also escaped damage. Ehlers immediately set up a heavy machine gun battery to protect the site. It was also around this time, on the morning of 17 June, that he found me and said: '*Siegfried, a bottle of Champers! I have just been awarded the Dödel, (a slang term applied to the Ritterkreuz).*' At the time he had 52 victories, including 20 *Viermots*. Several days later, two Mosquitos flew over the airfield. Flying at a height of 50 metres, they dropped six bombs. Ehlers told us not to disturb the craters; the *Staffeln*, passing to the left and right of them, could still take-off and land. A sensible instruction because Mosquitos frequently passed over our camouflaged installations without realising our activities continued."

On 17 June, 7./JG 51 lost three pilots during a combat with about 20 Mustangs near Alençon. The fact that a mechanic was found wedged behind the seat in one of the Fw 190s indicated that this small unit was moving to a new base. Two P-51s were claimed during this combat by the *Staffelführer*. But that day was to see further problems; the Eighth Air Force launched a fresh series of attacks on airfields used by German units. Lonrai and Essay were among the targets. The latter was badly damaged, and II. *Gruppe* was forced to move to Semallé several kilometres distant.

Leutnant Fritz Wegner, of 5./JG 1, recalls: "We put in a lot of effort in getting our airfield into shape. Things were not yet finished when, on 17 June, a new attack caught us by surprise. The *Viermots* were flying due south. We thought they were heading for Paris. Suddenly someone shouted: '*Listen, that noise is getting louder!*' We then saw the enemy aircraft execute a turn and fly right over the airfield from the south. At that moment, I was sitting on a case of bombs discussing our next mission. I shouted: '*Everyone head over to the south of the airfield!*' The men jumped into a vehicle, which took off like a whirlwind! I was unable to catch it up. I was trapped, and was soon joined by an old soldier. We had only a few seconds to get as far away as possible from our own bombs. We were going to feel enough of them! Hardly had we flattened ourselves on the ground than the heavens opened on us. An eternity later, we were still alive, but in a different world. Everything was in chaos. Our case of bombs had 'evaporated'! An hour passed before the men returned. They did not think they would find us alive."

Lt. Günther Heckmann of 7./JG 51: "After changing base, our formation was dispersed in the Alençon region. My *Schwarm* settled in the grounds of a chateau. There were four pilots and we lodged in tents near the aircraft, which were hidden in a wood. On the other side of the airfield another *Schwarm* led the same lifestyle. Three or four times a day the telephone would ring with orders for a mission. The experience gained on the eastern front was beneficial; there we had always fought in small formations against the elite pilots of the Red Guard. We quickly learned the rules for survival in Normandy. Mustangs and Thunderbolts continually circled and dived as soon as they saw their prey. The only possibility of escaping them was to bank and engage them in a turning dogfight. Nerves of steel were required. Pilots who tried to flee had no chance; the Americans would catch them in seconds. Typhoons, Tempests and Spitfires were the aircraft which were capable of dogfighting. Combat was more 'equal' than on the Russian Front even if the enemy were superior by five or six times. The *Flak* which covered the Invasion fleet was impressive, but it was nothing compared to that which protected Leningrad. The Allies profited from the quantity of their materials; the Russians used what they had with remarkable precision."

On 20 June, as the US First Army approached Cherbourg, II./JG 1 and its supplementary *Staffel*, 7./JG 51, joined up with I. *Gruppe*. At 08.30 hrs, eight Fw 190 A-8s of 7./JG 51 and four from I. *Gruppe* took off for a *freie-Jagd* mission over the coast. A clash with Lightnings ensued. *Uffz.* Walter Dobrath recorded his fourth and fifth victories, the latter coming as a result of colliding with a P-38. Three other Lightnings were claimed, *Lt.* Siegfried Stoffel being among the claimants. However, several German pilots were lost. Dobrath's fourth victory was probably a Lightning from the 370th Fighter Group piloted by Lieutenant Robert Rice. This Lightning became separated during the engagement and there was no American witness to what happened. The aircraft crashed between

Trun and Gacé, in the Argentan area. The fifth victory, which could only have been an accident, came shortly afterwards near Nonant-le-Pin. The victim, a Lightning from the same unit, was piloted by Lieutenant Roger. H. Wainwright. Lieutenant Lawrence Watson, who took part in the combat, remembered: "We were returning from an armed reconnaissance mission in the Le Mans region when our attention was drawn to enemy aircraft at seven o'clock. Coming out of the sun, they dived towards us. We took up defensive positions. Lieutenant Wainwright and myself turned towards the first Fw 190. I fired for ten seconds and then changed course. At that moment I saw a P-38 and a Fw 190 in flames diving towards the ground, the two left wings locked together. A parachute emerged, and I was convinced it was a German pilot. The two aircraft disappeared under the cloud base at 4,265 ft (1,300 m)."

Apart from the Fw 190 attributed to Wainwright, Lawrence Watson, Lieutenant Horace Plummer and Captain James Gordy of 370th Fighter Group each claimed a Fw 190.

Lt. Siegfried Stoffel achieved his fifth victory in Normandy on 22 June when he shot down a Thunderbolt, but he was killed in action the following day at around 22.00 hrs near Alençon, during combat with 20 P-47s. During the afternoon of 23 June, *Ofw.* Rudolf Hübl recorded his 19th and last victory with JG 1. His formation of eight machines attacked two P-51s near Caen at 15.30 hrs. One German and one American aircraft went down.

In I. *Gruppe*, Dobrath was wounded, Stoffel killed and Hübl was wounded by *Flak* on 27 June. Rathofer was killed three days later after raising his Normandy score to five. Aircraft losses were heavy; by the evening of 30 June, I. *Gruppe* could only count on four serviceable Fw 190s.

With II. *Gruppe* things were not much better. Shortly after arriving at Semallé, they suffered a further attack. On 25 June, at about 13.00 hrs, 15 Mustangs (although other reports say Thunderbolts) strafed the airfield and destroyed 15 Fw 190s. These aircraft proved difficult to replace.

The same evening, 20 pilots took off in a Ju 52 and a He 111 bound for Köln-Ostheim to seek out replacement Fw 190s. II. *Gruppe* was therefore out of action until mid-July. During this period, *Oblt.* Georg-Peter Eder, *Staffelkapitän* of 6. *Staffel*, was awarded a well-deserved *Ritterkreuz*. He had 49 victories to his credit, the last being over a P-47 near Le Mans on 21 June. On 1 July, he was promoted to *Hauptmann* and transferred to JG 26.

These promotions and awards were a necessary psychological boost. June had been a catastrophic month for the *Luftwaffe*. After three weeks of combat, it was on its knees. The Allies claimed the destruction of over 1,000 German aircraft. In numerous units, many of the few experienced pilots had gone.

On 4 July, 11 Fw 190 A-8s of I. *Gruppe* and 7./JG 51 took off shortly before 14.00 hrs. They met the US 404th Fighter Group over Coutances. Combat was joined and three German pilots were shot down. Two were from 7./JG 51, including the *Staffelführer*, the Austrian *Lt.* Friedrich 'Kraksel' Krakowitzer, who had 25 victories, most of them claimed in the East.

I. *Gruppe* was grateful for the acquisition of an additional *Staffel*, the 9. *Staffel* from JG 77. Led by *Oblt.* Wolfgang Ernst, 9./JG 77 joined I. *Gruppe* at Lonrai. Conversion training from the Bf 109 to the Fw 190 had been poor; on average six hours flying per pilot, part of which was taken up with flying with a 250 kg (55 lb) bomb. On 6 July, four pilots from 9./JG 77 carried out their first mission over Normandy. In conjunction with seven other aircraft, they took off at 15.35 hrs for a patrol in the Nogent-le-Rotrou/Mamers area. The 9./JG 77 *Schwarm* suddenly found itself in the presence of four P-38s of the American 428th Fighter Squadron which were providing top cover for the 429th, who were simultaneously undertaking a strafing mission. A short and violent combat ensued. Hurriedly, Captain John Hewitt, leading the American unit, ordered his pilots to break off combat in view of the presence of the other Fw 190s. However, two of his P-38s had already been shot down in flames, by *Oblt.* Ernst and *Fw.* Loch. Simultaneously, an Fw 190 was shot down, and shortly afterwards another. The two German victims were *Uffz.* Maximow and his *Staffelkapitän*, *Oblt.* Ernst, who described the end of the engagement: "I had just shot down a P-38 when I, in turn, was hit. I had to bale out but I waited until the last second before jumping; we all knew the Americans did not hesitate in machine-gunning our pilots when hanging from their parachutes. I got out of the cockpit, and the air current caught me and I hit the rudder. My right arm was broken with the impact. Shortly afterwards,

The toll mounts. Most of the Fw 190 A-8s belonging to II./JG 1 were destroyed on the ground at Semallé on 25 June 1944 by Allied fighter-bombers. The unit's pilots subsequently returned to Germany to collect new aircraft.

the parachute canopy opened and I eventually landed. My misgivings had not disappeared, since a group of civilians were heading towards the wood where I landed. *Maquis*? If they were, they were coming to finish me off. By chance, German Field Police arrived and the locals disappeared."

Ernst's assailant was Lt. Robert C Milliken in a P-38J-10 of the 429th Fighter Squadron. Milliken recalls: "We were alternately providing top cover as we worked our way back to the coast, approaching an area we identified as being near Nogent. The weather was clear, though I seem to remember a few clouds. I was number four in Lt. Paul Munger's flight – I was on Bill Bank's right wing as he was number three. I first saw minute tracers and then two explosions and then the planes involved came in view. I saw one P-38 in a dogfight with four Fw 190s.

"We climbed to 10,000 feet and attacked. There was a parachute in the air. Banks caught a 190 with a deflection shot at very close range and it went down in flames. A 190 attacked us from five o'clock. I called for Banks to break right, but he was occupied calling to Munger; he was calling '*I got one Munger, I got one!*'"

"I had to leave Banks and break right into a tight turn with the 190. I was equipped with a 'G' Suit for the first time and with combat flaps down and full throttle, I was turning inside him and I began to pull my sights through him. I had to leave him as a second 190 came in at about 5 o'clock. I set up a right turn with him and in about a 360 degree turn, I pulled my sights through him and fired a short burst. He rolled left into a split-S. I rolled into a dive to follow him. I was in a near vertical dive and I could see the 190 several thousand feet below.

"I looked to my left and a 190 was firing at the individual in the chute. It appeared that he did not hit him. As the attacker passed the chute, I turned into him and he started a right turn towards me. I cut him off with a short burst and he dived. I followed him and as I approached him we were at a low altitude. I realized that I was going to overshoot him. I had to make a climbing left 360. I timed it so that I felt I could out-turn him if he chose to set up a turning encounter. As I set up my turn, I could not see him and as I completed the turn (I was doing a 360, but I felt my head did a 720), I found that he had flown to the right and was skimming some tree tops three or four hundred yards away.

"I turned to follow and as I closed the distance between us, he hit the deck and flew up and over a power line. I saw this coming and just cleared the top of the power line and as I closed further, our props were skimming the ground. He then flew over a hay stack. I cleared both of these obstacles and was firing an occasional burst. He then flew over a small grove of trees to the right and as he cleared the trees, he climbed sharply to the left to about 500 feet and leveled out. I was closing rapidly and firing short bursts. As I closed, he

ABOVE LEFT: Ofw. Friedrich Zander of 8./JG 1 at La Fère, July 1944. Zander claimed five victories on the Invasion Front.

ABOVE: Ground personnel listen intently as Ofw. Friedrich Zander recounts his last mission in front of his Bf 109, 'Blue 22'.

BELOW: Lt. Robert C. Milliken of the 429th Fighter Squadron stands in front of his P38J-25 'Eileen' in late August 1944. In July, Milliken had shot down Obl. Wolfgang Ernst of 9./JG 77 which had been seconded to JG 1.

ABOVE AND ABOVE RIGHT: *Ofw.* and *Ritterkreuzträger* Herbert Kaiser of 7./JG 1 about to climb out of his Bf 109 'Blue 23' at La Fère. On 12 and 13 *July*, he claimed two victories on the Invasion Front.

RIGHT: *Lt.* Hans Düsterbeck (III./JG 1's Intelligence Officer) converses with *Fw.* and *Ritterkreuzträger* Herbert Kaiser (back to camera) at La Fère, *July* 1944.

jettisoned his canopy. I could see his black flight helmet, his tan flight suit and the stark white of his chute webbing. He jumped out to the left on the wing. I was about 75 yards away and firing. I chose not to fire at him – I could have blown him away – and directed my tracers to the right. He opened his chute and the force of the chute opening pulled him off the wing and he passed directly under me.

"I wanted to get the final flight of the 190 on film. I did not have time to switch to camera only, so I kept firing as I followed and the 190 half-rolled to the right and dived to the ground. It hit the earth in flames at Montmerrei, eight miles NNE of Alençon and skidded along the ground parallel to some growth or fence line. I had fired such a long burst that I had burnt out my cannon and guns and as I pulled up to the right my cannon kept cooking off three or four rounds.

"On August 6, 1944 we moved from our base at Warmwell in England to France at 'A-11', two miles south of Isigny. On August 24 James S. Frederick came to my tent to see me. I was on leave in Paris or London. Frederick was the pilot who had parachuted. He wanted to thank me for shooting down the 190 which had been strafing him. He had witnessed much of my battle as he was descending and landing with his chute. He told my tent mates that he had attempted to shoot the enemy as he landed close to him. However he said he could not cock his 45 as his hands were burnt."

For his part, *Oblt.* Ernst underwent long months of recovery, then moved to JG 53. In the meantime almost all of the personnel of 9./JG 77 had been posted missing.

The following day, 7 July, 9./JG 77 was renamed 4./JG 1. *Lt.* Gerhard Hanf, who took over from *Oblt.* Ernst, shot down his first Thunderbolt of the campaign (he was to claim another on 30 July).

At 13.10 hrs on 5 July, III./JG 1 left Wunstorf and returned to the front via Wiesbaden and Metz. Its strength was again up to 50 pilots, but they were of doubtful quality due to inexperience. The officer strength of the unit was weakened by the malaria which struck *Oblt.* Lutz-Wilhelm Burkhardt, *Staffelkapitän* of 7. *Staffel*. Burkhardt was replaced by *Oblt.* Fritz Bilfinger, formerly of JG 52.

On 11 July, III./JG 1 landed at the airstrip at La Fère joining *Stab* JG 1. The first *Freie-Jagd* and ground-strafing missions were initiated with considerable vigour and commitment – two, three or sometimes even four missions per day for each pilot. Results from the first day were encouraging; a P-51 was shot down by *Uffz.* Vogel without loss, but the hard reality of life in Normandy returned the next day. On 12 July, two officers of the *Gruppe*, *Hptm.* Friedrich Kasuhn and *Oblt.* Heinz Lammich, both former bomber pilots who had converted to fighters, were killed near Caen. *Lt.* Kurt Ibing, formerly of II. *Gruppe*, was wounded. By contrast, *Kommodore* Ihlefeld recorded a 'hat-trick' when three Spitfires fell to his guns. *Uffz.* Moser and *Oblt.* Bilfinger claimed a P-51 each and *Ofw.* Kaiser, a Spitfire.

On the 13th, towards 20.00 hrs, an element from JG 1 encountered a formation of Spitfires, Typhoons and Thunderbolts. One German pilot was killed; however two Typhoons were shot down by two of the most experienced pilots of the unit, *Hptm.* Grislawski and *Ofw.* Kaiser.

On the 14th, *Geschwaderstab* and III./JG 1 faired even better when no fewer than eight enemy fighters fell under its guns. Ihlefeld claimed a P-51 and a Spitfire, Woitke, a P-47 and Grislawski, a P-51.

During this period, II./JG 1 rebuilt its strength. With about 40 Fw 190s based principally at Semallé and Lonrai, the *Gruppe* once again undertook combat operations. On the 14th, *Fw.* Alfred Bindseil of 6./JG 1 claimed a Spitfire and a P-51, while three P-47s (including two credited to *Uffz.* Paul Taube) were shot down by 4./JG 1 (formerly 9./JG 77).

On the 17th, III. *Gruppe* claimed four Spitfires and the next day, two further Spitfires and three P-38s by *Obstlt.* Ihlefeld, *Hptm.* Woitke and *Fw.* Pleines. But the *Gruppe* lost three pilots killed in action and one wounded. The latter was *Kommandeur* Woitke who was forced into taking dangerous low-level evasive action by a formation of P-38 Lightnings. Unable to avoid striking a tree near Pont-Laverne, he desperately climbed for a few seconds so as to gain sufficient height from which to jump. However, the violent opening of his parachute dislocated both his shoulders. Sent to hospital, he would rejoin his unit with his chest encased in plaster.

The 19th saw a major success for III. *Gruppe*. No fewer than seven Typhoons and one Spitfire were shot down east of Caen at around 21.00 hrs. Among the seven victorious pilots were *Hptm.* Grislawski, *Uffz.* Hausotter, both of 8. *Staffel*. and *Oblt.* Bilfinger who was accredited with the Spitfire.

At 12.30 hrs on 20 July, 30 aircraft from II./JG 1 were airborne. Flying at 700 m (2,300 ft) over the Bérigny area, the formation was bounced by Spitfires and Thunderbolts. Seven pilots were lost, either killed, missing or taken prisoner, for only three Spitfires shot down, these accredited to *Ofw.* Reinhard Flecks and *Oblt.* Rüdiger von Kirchmayr (2). During the evening a pilot from 7./JG 51, *Gefr.* Johannes Kamutzki, was also lost during a transfer flight from Alençon to Le Mans.

In the early evening of 23 July, 40 P-38s of the 370th Fighter Group were returning from a mission against the marshalling yards at Limours when they encountered 10 Fw 190s from II./JG 1. Fierce combat ensued between Etampes and the area south of Versailles. Four P-38s were shot down and their pilots killed. The Fw 190 A-7 of *Uffz.* Erich Rahner of 7./JG 51 was behind that of *Ofw.* Leo Schuhmacher. Glancing into his rear view mirror, Schuhmacher realised that something was wrong; Rahner appeared out of control and his undercarriage was partly lowered. Schuhmacher shouted to the unfortunate pilot over the radio to make a wheels-up landing. The resulting impact was so severe that Rahner was in a coma for three days. Schuhmacher belly-landed alongside his comrade. He enlisted the help of some local civilians and two soldiers to wrench the canopy off, save Rahner and take him to hospital in Chartres. It appeared that Rahner had lost consciousness due to fumes from the auxiliary fuel tank seeping into the cockpit.

On 24 July, two pilots of 7. *Staffel* were killed in action against Spitfires near Caen. But *Ofw.* Hans Kaniss of 8. *Staffel* recorded two victories over P-38s in another combat.

On 25 July, the Allied air forces launched a large attack designed to break up German ground forces and introduce more flexibility to the Allied armies. A patrol from III./JG 1 attacked a formation of Spitfires over Lisieux. Three were shot down before a further three were claimed by I./JG 5.

Uffz. Hugo Hausotter of 8./JG 1: "We took off from La Fère heading towards Caen at 10.28 hours. After about 30 minutes, Spitfires came out of the sun and opened fire. We promptly jettisoned our auxiliary tanks and retaliated. We shot down several Spitfires including one for me, which was my second victory. A few seconds later, my Messerschmitt was hit and burst into flames. I jumped out at the very last possible moment. It was at 11.05. Some military police came to my rescue and took me back to La Fère where the burns to my face were treated. On 2 August, following a week of medical care, I went back into action."

III./JG 1 launched at least two further missions on 25 July. They would bring claims of three P-47s and a P-51 at 16.00 hrs, as well as a Lancaster and a Spitfire shot down by *Obstlt.* Ihlefeld around 19.30 hrs. Nevertheless, the day cost III./JG 1 the loss of three pilots wounded and an equivalent number killed in the skies between Rouen and Caen. Among the latter, were *Oblt.* Wolfgang Meyer, a very experienced bomber pilot recently posted to III./JG 1.

On 27 July, *Obstlt.* Ihlefeld shot down a P-51 shortly before 19.30 hrs. *Fw.* Fritz Haspel of 8. *Staffel* was hit in the left arm by a burst of cannon fire. He managed to bale out but injured his legs on landing. Helped by a local woman on the ground, he was handed over to German soldiers and taken to hospital. Haspel would only return to his *Gruppe* in December 1944. His *Staffel* comrade, *Uffz.* Werner Moser, also had to bale out

Three officers of III./JG 1 relax in the shade of the trees at La Fère, July 1944; Dr Bernd Kettner (Gruppe doctor), Hptm. Frank Marschall (Gruppeadjutant) and Oblt. Erich Buchholz (a former pilot of 5./JG 1 who later became Gruppenadjutant of III./JG 1 and Staffelkapitän of 9./JG 1).

and was not so lucky; his wounds would keep him from the front until February 1945.

The month of July had cost III. *Gruppe* around 20 pilots killed or wounded, mainly in the Caen area. In total, the unit claimed approximately 50 victories.

The situation for I. *Gruppe* was critical; on 25 July the unit did not have a single Fw 190 on strength. Thirty pilots were sent to Köln to take delivery of new aircraft. Pilots and aircraft would return to France two days later. On 30 July, I. and II. *Gruppen* reinforced by new *Staffeln* from JG 51 and JG 77 claimed nine P-47s (among these two for *Ofw.* Reinhard Flecks) and a Spitfire for the loss of three pilots killed or missing in action and four wounded.

ABOVE: A former pilot of II. and III./JG 1 and Oesau's favoured wingman, Fw. Rudolf Rauhaus was posted to Stab I./JG 1 shortly before operations commenced over the Invasion Front. He was killed near Caen on 31 July 1944.

LEFT: A Schwarm from 9./JG 1 in the summer sky over France, 1944.

MIDDLE LEFT AND RIGHT: Uffz. Jakob Vogel's Bf 109 G-6 'Black 7' (W.Nr. 413601) of 8./JG 1, captured by the British after an emergency landing near Fontenay-le-Pesnel on 22 July 1944.

LEFT: Fw 190 A-8 'Black 5' crashed in Normandy. It is probably the aircraft of Obgfr. Max-Ulrich Förster of 2./JG 1 who was posted missing near St. Lô on 28 July 1944.

"Indescribable chaos..." **257**

Messerschmitt Bf 109 G-6 'Yellow 2'
8./JG 1
La Fère
July 1944

LEFT AND BELOW: Bf 109 G-6 'Yellow 2' of 8./JG 1 landing at La Fère.

BELOW: An almost peaceful scene at La Fère during the Summer of 1944. A Bf 109 G-6 is towed towards the shelter of trees.

On the morning of 25 July 1944, Uffz. Hugo Hausotter of 8./JG 1 shot down a Spitfire in his Bf 109 G-6/AS 'Black 14' but had to bale out a few seconds later after being hit himself. These photographs were taken at La Fère the same month.

Messerschmitt Bf 109 G-6/AS 'Black 14'
Uffz. Hugo Hausotter
8./JG 1
La Fère
July 1944

Chapter Nineteen

"Enemy fighters were always lying in wait…"

Retreat – August 1944

Until 1 August 1944, German forces in Normandy had succeeded in containing the Allies in the Cotentin Peninsula. However, the front had broken the day before and the US 4th Armored Division swept south through von Choltitz's 84th Corps to take Avranches. American units then thrust northwards, encircling significant German forces in the Falaise pocket. The defence of France was crumbling; the route to the Seine and Paris was open. The French capital was liberated on 25 August.

For the *Jagdwaffe*, by now bled almost white, there was no hope of remaining in France. On the ground, Allied forces were advancing rapidly towards their airfields and the need for total evacuation drew ever nearer. But neither fuel nor replacement aircraft were coming through. The sky was black with Allied aircraft. German fighters were run to ground everywhere.

At the beginning of August, at Lonrai, I./JG 1 could call only upon 11 serviceable Fw 190 A-8s. On 4 and 5 August, the *Gruppe* moved to Oysonville where it carried out two to three sorties per day. On 7 August, at 14.10 hrs, 15 Fw 190 A-8s took off on a ground attack mission to the Courandes area. The formation was intercepted by American fighters. Four German pilots were killed and one, the experienced *Ofw.* Hans Kaniss, wounded. Four hours later, several machines of I. and II./JG 1 took off and exacted revenge by shooting down three P-47s, one falling to the guns of *Lt.* Emil Demuth, *Staffelkapitän* of 3. *Staffel*. On 11 August, I. *Gruppe* left Oysonville for Aulnay-aux-Planches, from where limited operations were conducted. On 22 August, they returned to Schleswig-Holstein in Germany for a period of rest. It is difficult to arrive at an accurate balance sheet for I. *Gruppe's* action in Normandy. However, it is known that the unit lost around 40 pilots either killed, wounded or taken prisoner, and claimed an approximately similar number of *Abschüsse*.

During the Normandy campaign, II. *Gruppe* lost 15 pilots, most of these during a bitter combat over St. Lô on 20 July. In August, missions became increasingly rare as the *Gruppe* retreated progressively eastwards.

Oblt. Rüdiger von Kirchmayr was *Staffelkapitän* of 5./JG 1: "On 11 August 1944, II./JG 1 moved to Connantre and from there, returned to Reinsehlen. However, a little earlier, a Mustang forced me to make an emergency wheels-up landing near Nogent. The smoothness of my landing was brutally interrupted by a hole and the shock knocked me out. An SS *Panzer* unit discovered me covered with blood and helped me to get out. They hauled me on to a tank and took me to Connantre, where a doctor wanted to hospitalise me for two weeks. With my *Gruppe* on the point of leaving for Reinsehlen, such immobilisation was inconceivable.

"With my head bandaged in a large dressing – which prevented me from using my radio – and thanks to the technicians in the rearguard, I was able to take off from Connantre the next day. They got ready to start up our last two machines, the first being grounded due to a damaged engine and the second suffering from damaged propeller blades.

"Assisted by three barely qualified men, I undertook to replace the damaged propeller blade on Fw 190 'Black 3' with one from the other machine. We worked through the night so as not to be seen by my doctor. In the morning, the machine was ready. I decided to fly to Störmede; I knew this airfield better than Reinsehlen and, furthermore, I knew that the female auxiliaries there would give me a good welcome!

"Flying at an altitude of 1,000m in splendid weather, I was attacked by a pair of Mustangs around Reims. How did I think I could have flown around like a tourist? This is incomprehensible to me today. The height of stupidity! A swirling combat began. But with my bad head, it was worth me finding a solution quickly so as to wriggle out of the situation. It seems that I was a pretty tough adversary for the two Mustangs. I hit one so hard, that his friends chose to break off their

Two Leutnante of II./JG 1 photographed on the steps of the château which served as their Gefechtsstand; Hubert Swoboda of 5./JG 1 and Helmut Weissbrodt of 7./JG 51.

RIGHT: Seen at Reinsehlen in late August 1944 are from right to left: Ofw. Hutter, Uffz. Weichard, Lt. Swoboda, Ofw. Flecks, unknown, unknown and Lt. Kremer (in light-coloured summer flight jacket).

ABOVE: Sorely tested during the Normandy campaign, II./JG 1 returned to Reinsehlen in August 1944 to 'rest and re-equip'. Here, the Gruppenkommandeur is in discussion with his commanding officers. In the foreground (from left to right): Lt. Otto Bach (7./JG 1), Hptm. Hermann Staiger (Gruppenkommandeur), Oblt. Fritz Wegner (6./JG 1), Hptm. Wolfgang Ludewig (8./JG 1) and Lt. Hubert Swoboda (5./JG 1).

engagement. I continued on my way, but this time, at ground level.

"At Störmede, I ran into Ofw. Otto Bach who had also returned alone. He had chosen this course for the same reasons as me. We celebrated our reunion with some very potent alcohol until midday on 24 August! By then, it was high time to leave again, because our unit was trying very hard to make contact with us through different sources. Having learned of my state, the Gruppenstab dispatched an ambulance, a doctor and some firemen along the runway in case there were any snags.

"On 8 September, I was once again declared fit for service, but a little after that, I was appointed Gruppenkommandeur of I./JG 11. On 19 September, I took off for the last time in my capacity as Staffelkapitän of 5./JG 1."

In contrast to II./JG 1, III. Gruppe remained very active for the whole of August. It was placed under the control of the Geschwaderstab, JG 27 along with II./JG 6 and II./JG 11. Herbert Kaiser of 7. Staffel recalled: "We were regularly in action against the fighter-bombers attacking our ground troops. Take-offs were carried out in small formations (two to four aircraft), since enemy fighters were always lying in wait above the clouds over our airfields. We only ever flew at a few metres above ground level, and more than one aircraft smashed into one of the small hills in the area. We only gained height when preparing to attack. One day, one of my three fellow pilots warned of a formation of Spitfires in the area. Just as we got into attack position, we were attacked ourselves by a second formation which shot down my companions in seconds. By chance, but also thanks to my experience, I escaped them."

In August, III. Gruppe would prove that the successes gained during both the previous two months had neither exhausted it nor diminished its abilities. Though its results during the ensuing Reichsverteidigung were sometimes lacklustre, operating conditions – and thus results – in Normandy seemed to be much better for the Gruppe.

On 1 August, three P-51s and a Spitfire were claimed by III./JG 1 whilst led by Ihlefeld. The mission saw him claim his ninth and final victory in Normandy. Similarly, the Spitfire was the fifth and last Abschuss for Lt. Franz Koplik of 9./JG 1. Koplik was shot down and killed by Mustangs the next day.

Ofhr. Hubert Heckmann, of 9./JG 1 recalls events after the mission: "On my return, I noticed that Buchholz and Oberarzt Kettner were walking up and down the edge of the woods deep in conversation. Next day, we were informed about the subject of the conversation; Buchholz had got a temporary take-off prohibition. The reason – combat was tough and crashes were increasing. Buchholz's wife was heavily pregnant and so if he crashed, such news could cause damage to mother and baby. The thing with Buchholz was that he'd had a lot of bad luck with the aircraft he chose. We guessed that he had had to drop out of every third mission due to mechanical problems. Every time this happened, he got words of farewell from those pilots who continued with the mission. They – we – sent a malicious '*Ha Ha*' over the radio whenever he turned back. *Hptm.* Woitke had broken his shoulder on a parachute jump and wore a '*Stuka*' (plaster cast). Therefore, Buchholz took on the administration on the ground. Because he didn't participate in missions any more, he also didn't suffer from the '*Ha Has*' because he didn't need to shirk any more."

On 5 August, III. *Gruppe* moved to Brétigny. The following day, 12 aircraft took off at 11.45 hrs heading for Paris to intercept a formation of 100 Lancasters escorted by nearly 150 fighters. Only four pilots returned. *Fj.Ofw.* Herbert Kaiser, a *Ritterkreuzträger* with 68 victories – of which six had been gained with JG 1 – had to bale out. Colliding with the rudder, he was seriously injured. A series of operations and subsequent convalescence kept him away from the front until February 1945. Three pilots were victorious; *Ofw.* Friedrich Zander (a Lancaster), *Ofw.* Leo-Lothar Barann (a Spitfire) and *Uffz.* Wilhelm Kräuter (a Spitfire). *Oblt.* Fritz Bilfinger, *Kapitän* of 7./JG 1 claimed a P-47 three hours later during a *freie-Jagd*.

At 19.30 hrs on 7 August, a pair of P-47s was claimed by two pilots of 7. *Staffel*; *Oblt.* Bilfinger and *Uffz.* Kräuter. This combat took place only a short time before one involving I. *Gruppe*. I./JG 1 sent its nine operational Fw 190s on one of its last missions in France. Again, results were good; *Lt.* Demuth and *Uffz.* Oswald of 3./JG 1 claimed a P-47 each and another fell to *Uffz.* Meyer of 9./JG 77. There were no losses.

Around 14:15 hrs on 10 August, *Ofw.* Friedrich Zander and *Uffz.* Hugo Hausotter, both of 8. *Staffel,* claimed victories over two British fighters, thought to be Typhoons, 45 minutes after having taken off from Brétigny, Hausotter scoring his third and final victory. As with his second victory, Hausotter had to bail out several seconds after.

On 12 August, *Hptm.* Grislawski recorded his last victory with JG 1 – a Spitfire. Next day, he received orders to leave III./JG 1 to take up an appointment as a *Staffelkapitän* with JG 53. The wounded *Hptm.* Erich Woitke was replaced by a pilot returning from convalescence, a veteran of the unit, *Hptm.* Heinz Knoke. Knoke was surprised to hear that he would be succeeding his old boss from the days when they served in II./JG 52 in 1941. The surprise was even greater when Knoke found out that Woitke had received no promotion since those days, in spite of having had numerous victories, though he was also well aware of Woitke's 'colourful' character and the problems that this had caused. It had been a long time since *Hptm.* Knoke had slung bombs under his fighter and attacked B-17s in 1943! (See *Defenders of the Reich, Volume Two*). As *Staffelkapitän* in JG 11, he had shown many of the required qualities since being given command, and to date had accumulated nearly 30 victories, including 19 *Viermots*. At the end of April 1944, he had been wounded in combat and was not yet fully recovered. Nevertheless, it did not stop him recording a further seven victories and becoming one of the highest scorers of the Normandy theatre.

As Knoke recorded: "During the night of 13-14 August, I reached my new *Gruppe's* base by car. To my surprise, I met up with my first commanding officer from the Eastern campaign, *Hauptmann* Woitke. He received me most warmly. The heavy strapping he had around his left shoulder and his body made him look like a medieval horseman. From the morning of the 14th, I was in action with my new unit, and during a combat with six Thunderbolts near Rennes I managed to hit one, which exploded in mid-air. On the way home, we attacked a column of enemy vehicles. I set

LEFT: Members of II./JG 1 in front of one of the unit's Fw 190 A-8s in the Summer of 1944. On the right is probably Ofw. Reinhard Flecks.

BELOW: Hptm. Alfred Grislawski, Staffelkapitän of 8./JG 1, left the unit at the end of the Normandy campaign to become Staffelkapitän of 11./JG 53. He was wounded in combat on 26 September 1944.

a Jeep on fire. On the 15th, we carried out an escort to fighter-bombers and in the ensuing combat, I scored my 28th victory, over a Thunderbolt. On the 16th, Spitfires attacked our base. I took off in pursuit and managed to shoot one down near Etampes."

On 17 August, Knoke shot down a Lightning near the village of Auxonette, and later in the day a Marauder, with three more claimed by his comrades. On the 18th, two Mustangs near Lisieux were added to his score.

"On 27 August, in six unsuccessful attacks against heavily defended pontoon bridges over the Seine, we lost 12 aircraft. The next day, we had only six operational, of which two were in a poor state. I flew one of them, my Adjutant, *Obergefreiter* Döring took the other. Unfortunately, he crashed on take-off and was killed. Eventually we engaged about 60 Mustangs and Thunderbolts. My companions quickly disappeared and I found myself alone with my wingman, *Unteroffizier* Ickes, who stoically followed my desperate manoeuvres to shake off a pursuing Mustang. Using a risky manoeuvre, I was able to surprise him and turn the situation to my advantage. He went down in flames. Then came a terrible shaking! Debris from my victim hit my aircraft. I had no other option but to bale out. On the ground, I was able to pass myself off as an American to four *Maquisards*, and to eventually get back to our lines. The Allies had broken through near Soissons. That night we had to retreat towards Cerfontaine in Belgium. I found out that, sadly, Ickes also had to bale out but was machine-gunned on his parachute and was found dead on the ground."

Uffz. Ullrich Wagner of 11./JG 1 remembers the events: "On that day, Knoke, Ickes, Döring, Freydank and myself were in action. Döring placed himself in front of me for take-off, but I signalled to him that I would go before him. He only had a few more seconds to live; his left wing touched the ground, the aircraft turned over and exploded. By the time the groundcrew arrived, it was too late. We circled over the airfield, but his aircraft was just a heap of burning metal. The remaining aircraft joined up; I flew close to Knoke. We headed for Compiègne. At a height of 3,500 metres we sighted eight Mustangs, who first of all thought we were friendly aircraft. We turned left, and the enemy also turned. At a distance of between 400 and 500 metres they hit us with their first burst. My aircraft was hit but it wasn't too bad. Knoke and the others continued to circle while I, with four *Amis* on my tail, did a climbing turn. Thanks to the methanol injection in the engine, I gradually pulled away. Only the Mustang which had hit me continued the chase.

A Fw 190 A-8 of 5./JG 1 refuels, France, Summer 1944.

A Fw 190 A-8 of 5./JG 1 with a white spiral on its spinner in Normandy, Summer 1944.

However, he was not able to bring his guns to bear. I slowly regained my calm and saw that my comrades were in a situation from which it was difficult to escape. Americans were arriving from every direction. Lightnings... Thunderbolts... Suddenly, I dipped my aircraft – my 'Yellow 4' – and dived fast. I then found myself all alone – there were no enemy aircraft in the vicinity. A little farther away, the remains of two aircraft were burning on the ground. Heading for Reims, I descended to 1,000 metres and landed at the base. None of my companions were able to do likewise. On the ground, I checked the damage. My adversary had hit me seven times, including single hits in the radiator and propeller. The following night, Knoke returned to Vailly with his parachute under his arm."

Contrary to the recollections of these pilots, it was on 23 August that *Obgfr.* Döring was killed during take-off, and the 25th when the final Normandy combat for III. *Gruppe* took place in which *Hptm.* Knoke baled out and the unfortunate *Uffz.* Friedrich Ickes was shot while hanging defenceless on his parachute. *Hptm.* Knoke's victories were gained at a heavy cost; a conversation recorded between two prisoners of the unit captured in the latter part of August revealed that: *"Our Gruppenkommandeur recently carried out three missions. He shot down two Spitfires and a P-51, but each time he lost his No.2, No.3 and No.4."*

Chapter Twenty

"Achtung! Indianer behind us!"

Return to the Reich

"We were ten days on the road, staging via Köln and Hamburg, before reaching Husum. At this time we received young pilots to fill the gaps following the last campaign. Generally, they were little more than boys. Each day, our chief would take the *Staffeln* into the air in different formations – *Rotte*, *Schwarm*, *Staffel* and *Gruppe*. Everything had to be taught to these youngsters, who arrived with only a few hours' flying time. Ehlers, our *Gruppenkommandeur*, was very diplomatic with the Mayor and population of Husum; they had to understand and accept the noise." So recalled *Hptm*. Ludwig Siegfried, *Oberzahlmeister* of I./JG 1.

At the beginning of October 1944, *Stab* and I. *Gruppe* was at Husum (Greifswald from 7 October) with Fw 190 A-8s and composed as follows:

Stab	*Hauptmann* Hans Ehlers
1. Staffel	*Leutnant* Hans-Joachim Luepke
2. Staffel	*Oberleutnant* Hans Vermaaten
3. Staffel	*Oberleutnant* Emil Demuth
4. Staffel	*Leutnant* Gerhard Hanf

Lt. Herbert Neuner, 2. *Staffel*, remembered of this time: "Recovered from my wounds suffered on 22 April 1944, I rejoined my 2. *Staffel* on 1 September at Husum. Gottfried Just was the only friend I found there. Like myself, he had been promoted to *Leutnant* during the summer. All the other pilots were inexperienced, even the *Staffel* leader, *Oberleutnant* Hans Vermaaten. All our time was dedicated to training. Eventually, we moved to a new base – Greifswald. During the transfer flight, *Oberleutnant* Vermaaten's wing touched the ground and the aircraft, carrying an auxiliary fuel tank, exploded. *Leutnant* Just took over the *Staffel*. We transformed the field at Greifswald into an excellent airstrip, with camouflaged pens in the woods for our Fw 190s. We continued with our exercises there."

II. *Gruppe* was established at Reinsehlen, in the Lüneburg area. Once again the unit operated from a field converted into an airfield. Fresh young pilots arrived to bring the *Gruppe* up to strength. The new *Gruppenkommandeur*, *Hptm*. Hermann Staiger, rejoined the *Gruppe* in mid-August in Normandy. He was an experienced pilot and former *Kommandeur* of I./JG 26, with around 60 victories. At the beginning of October, II. *Gruppe's* command structure was as follows:

Uffz. Friedrich Enderle of 3./JG 1 and his Fw 190 A-8 'Yellow 5' at Eggebek in September 1944. Note the all-leather flight suit which became common place in the Jagdwaffe at around this time.

Stab and II. *Gruppe* at Reinsehlen (Tutow from November) with Fw 190 A-8s

Stab	*Hauptmann* Hermann Staiger
5. Staffel	*Leutnant* Hubert Swoboda
6. Staffel	*Leutnant* Fritz Wegner
7. Staffel	*Leutnant* Otto Bach
8. Staffel	*Leutnant* Günther Heckmann.

Leutnant Karl-Heinz Sundermeier of III./JG 1 remembered the end in France: "On 23 August, I arrived at Vailly. On the runway, a Bf 109 was burnt out – a pilot had crashed on taking off. *Hauptmann* Grislawski, *Staffelkapitän* of 8. *Staffel*, had just left the unit and I was the only officer in the *Staffel*. I was also the youngest pilot. Three days after I arrived, we heard that the *Gruppe* had been disbanded. Accompanied by several other surviving pilots, I travelled to Beaurieux, where we were incorporated into 5. *Staffel*, *Jagdgeschwader* 11. This unit soon left French soil. On 1 September, after a short stop-over in Cerfontaine, Belgium, we landed at Wiesbaden. It was exactly five years since the war began, and we were evacuating France! II. *Gruppe*, *Jagdgeschwader* 11, was based on the airfield at Gymnich. Our small group of pilots from III. *Gruppe*, *Jagdgeschwader* 1, was assigned to an officer who had recently finished convalescing, *Oberleutnant* Fritz Bilfinger. After two combat missions from Gymnich, we moved to Breitschneid-Burbach in Westerwald. Not far away was Knoke and other remnants of III. *Gruppe*, *Jagdgeschwader* 1. Soon, we were moved to Wesel to oppose Allied paratroops in the Arnhem area. Finally, on 2 October 1944, we received the order to return to III. *Gruppe*, *Jagdgeschwader* 1, who were at Fels-am-Wagram, where they were building up strength. We then moved on to Anklam to take up combat again in defence of the *Reich*."

After being based in France and Belgium, *Hptm*. Heinz Knoke's *Gruppe* was transferred to Vienna. The unit left its remaining aircraft in the Reims area. Three days were spent in Austria, then a further move to Anklam ensued. The convoy only had a day and a half to cover a good 1,000 km (621 ml) over damaged roads with the added problem of finding food supplies. On 9 October 1944, III. *Gruppe* once again lost its *Gruppenkommandeur*. On the journey Knoke, driving a car, suffered a bad accident. He managed to avoid undergoing amputation to his leg, but his career as a pilot was over. It had been an illustrious career, which included 44 victories in the West (among them 19 four-engined and a Mosquito), and was rounded off with the award of one of the very last *Ritterkreuz* on 27 April 1945.

Recovered from his injuries, *Hptm.* Erich Woitke once again took command of the unit. The *Stab* and III. *Gruppe* was based at Anklam with Bf 109 G-10s as follows:

Stab	Hauptmann Erich Woitke
9. Staffel	Oberleutnant Helmut Müller
10. Staffel	Oberleutnant Fritz Bilfinger
11. Staffel	Oberleutnant Jochen Janke
12. Staffel	Hauptmann Harald Moldenhauer

In mid-November, the Allies were fighting on the frontiers of the *Reich*. In the air, the end of the fighting in France led to the return of the systematic bombing of targets in Germany.

Oblt. Hans-Joachim Janke, a former Zerstörer pilot, became Staffelkapitän of 11./JG 1 in October 1944.

The *Geschwader* was brought up to strength again with, remarkably, manpower never having been so high before, though there was, to a degree, a loss of quality. The enthusiasm of the young pilots was real enough, perhaps more so than before, but it was not enough to fill the gaps with pilots who had merely received accelerated training.

Once again, I. *Gruppe* had the difficult task of being the first to go into combat. On 21 November, at 10.42 hrs, in bad weather conditions, *Hptm.* Ehlers took off from Greifswald at the head of a formation of 56 Fw 190 A-8s. The USAAF sent nearly 1,300 *Viermots* with a quarter of the aircraft drawn from 1st Bomb Division. The Division had, as its objective, the synthetic oil refineries at Merseburg, 350 km (217 mls) to the south of Greifswald. They were escorted by 245 Mustangs out of a total of 968 American fighters committed that day. *Lt.* Herbert Neuner of 2. *Staffel* recalled: "On 21 November operations began again in dreadful weather; there was rain and fog. Our formation was directed due south towards a formation of *Viermots*. Suddenly, voices crackled over the intercom: *'Achtung! Indianer behind us!'* Our *Gruppe* was split up. I dived but was hit several times. Having noticed that I was not being followed, I climbed and saw a large circle of aircraft. In the circle aircraft were weaving, one behind the other. I picked up speed, got behind a P-47 and shot it down. I broke away immediately and set course for home. By chance, the route was good and I landed at Greifswald. If my memory is correct, only two or three of my companions joined me. We waited for further news. It was very bad; the absentees were posted missing and, hour by hour, their deaths were confirmed."

The losses were numerous. It took the Americans only one or two minutes to shoot down and kill eight of their adversaries over Erfurt. In the encounters which followed, seven more German pilots were killed and five wounded. Some 35 aircraft of I./JG 1 were lost. Only three victories were recorded over B-17s, one each to *Lt.* Demuth, *Ofhr.* Stiemer and *Uffz.* Enderle. As previously recounted, *Lt.* Neuner claimed a P-47, and *Fw.* Oswald and *Uffz.* Riehl one *Herausschuss* each.

On 26 November, the American air forces sent more than 1,000 bombers escorted by nearly 700 fighters against various railway and oil targets in the Ruhr area. I./JG 1, which could call only upon 32 Fw 190s, took off at 11.20 hrs led by *Lt.* Gottfried Just, who temporarily replaced Ehlers. II. *Gruppe* was also in action under the command of the *Staffelkapitän* of 7./JG 1, *Lt.* Otto Bach, who had replaced the *Kommandeur*; the latter's Fw 190 suffered engine problems and took off 20 minutes later. Once again, there were heavy losses. The intervention of the P-51 escort was very effective and nine pilots of II. *Gruppe* were killed, including Bach, who had been with JG 1 since the formation of IV. *Gruppe*. Three pilots, including the *Staffelführer* of 5./JG 1, *Lt.* Hubert Swoboda, were wounded. Only two B-24s were claimed – by *Hptm.* Staiger and *Lt.* Heckmann respectively. The *Geschwaderstab* and I. *Gruppe* each lost a pilot.

Tutow, November 1944. Reichsmarschall Hermann Göring visits II./JG 1 for the last time and takes the opportunity to award Ofw. Reinhard Flecks of 6./JG 1 the German Cross in Gold.

Two pilots of 2./JG 1 standing on the wing of a Fw 190 A-8 at Greifswald. To the left, Lt. Herbert Neuner (wounded in action on 23 December 1944) and right, Ofhr. Wilhelm Ade (wounded in action on 14 January 1945).

Uffz. Gerhard Hildenbrand of 11./JG 1 in his Bf 109 G.

USAAF Intelligence Officers later described the German fighter attacks launched that day as "*... viciously pressed.*"

On 5 December, matters reached a peak, or rather hit the depths. The complete *Geschwader* took off around 10.30 hrs. A force of 451 B-17s from the 1st and 3rd Bomb Divisions escorted by 711 Mustangs were paying a return visit to Berlin. I. *Gruppe* were able to put 42 Fw 190s into the air. By the evening, half of them would be written off. The loss list was appalling. I. *Gruppe*: 6 killed and 11 wounded; II. *Gruppe*: 14 killed and 2 wounded; III. *Gruppe*: 5 killed and 1 wounded. Among those killed were the new *Staffelführer* of 7. *Staffel*, *Oberleutnant* Rudolf Diesem, and *Oberleutnant* Helmut Müller, *Staffelführer* of 9. *Staffel*. I. *Gruppe* claimed nine Mustangs; *Leutnante* Neuner, Just and Luepke were among the victors. II. *Gruppe* claimed seven with *Hptm.* Staiger and *Ofw.* Flecks among the scorers. In III. *Gruppe*, *Hptm.* Moldenhauer and *Fw.* Hausotter recorded a victory each over P-51s. Once again, the *Luftwaffe* seems to have over-claimed – some 30 victories over Mustangs while the USAAF actually recorded losses of 'only' 15 aircraft over Europe. Some German claims were not real.

Lt. Ottokar Henning of 12./JG 1: "Two machines stayed on the ground when III./JG 1 took off; Bf 109 'Blue 3' belonging to my friend *Ofhr.* Hans-Werner Kroll and my own 'Blue 4'. Knowing that my friend's technical problem would be quickly resolved, I preferred to wait so that he would not have to attempt to catch up with the *Gruppe* alone. After five minutes, the technicians gave us the authorisation to take off. We quickly joined our friends. But combat started immediately and we were attacked from the rear. I succeeded in escaping by diving. But by then, Hans-Werner was already hit. I landed on a small airfield in the Loewenberg area. No one could give me any news of my unit. Back at Anklam, I learned that my friend had been killed. I borrowed a car and found the crash site. His machine was in a pitiful state. Several shell holes were visible. They had already taken his body away. Despite the fearful danger of the situation, *Hptm.* Moldenhauer managed to get a P-51 near Wittstock."

After a week of relative calm, events once again intensified. On 16 December, the Germans launched their last offensive in the West. Under cover of bad weather and using strong armoured forces, Hitler intended to break through in the Ardennes region, cross the Meuse and push on to Antwerp. The Allied forces in the region would be cut in two. Peace in the West might then ensue, allowing the Germans freedom to continue the battle in the East.

To this end, on 17 December, shortly before 10.00 hrs, I./JG 1 left Greifswald, its Fw 190s flying at low level and guided by a Ju 88. They landed at Twente. Only a small part of the airfield was useable. II. *Gruppe* reached Drope, and III. *Gruppe* took off from Anklam at 09.47 and took up residence at Rheine. During the Ardennes offensive, the *Geschwader's* high rate of attrition continued. On 18 December, towards 11.30 hrs, 28 Fw 190 A-8s of I. *Gruppe* were in action in the Malmédy region. One pilot was reported missing. At the same time, III. *Gruppe* encountered B-17s in the Köln-Bonn region. Several pilots were shot down and had to bale out, one of them seriously wounded. *Lt.* Hubert Heckmann of 12./JG 1 claimed his fifth kill over a P-51.

On the 23rd, towards midday, all of III./JG 1's serviceable aircraft (there were not more than 12) scrambled to intercept a flight of B-17s. *Oblt.* Jochen Janke, *Staffelkapitän* of 11./JG 1 shot down a B-17 in his first *Abschuss* but was then shot down himself by a P-51 and forced to bale out near Köln. *Hptm.* Erich Woitke claimed a *Herausschuss*, his last victory.

Two hours later, I. *Gruppe* went into action against a formation of P-47s. Three pilots were killed and one wounded: *Lt.* Neuner, hit by German *Flak*. The *Gruppe* recorded three Thunderbolts shot down by *Hptm.* Hans Ehlers, *Lt.* Herbert Neuner and *Lt.* Emil Demuth.

At 11:26 hrs on 24 December, III./JG 1 took off from Rheine and shortly afterwards lost its *Gruppenkommandeur*, *Hptm.* Erich Woitke, who was shot down by a Spitfire and remained in his Bf 109 G-14, 'Grey 20' until it crashed near Aachen. He was 33 years old, and had been accredited with 28 victories. He was succeeded by Hauptmann Harald Moldenhauer, the *Staffelkapitän* of 12. *Staffel*. *Lt.* Hans Halbey of Stab/III JG 1 recalled events: "Shortly after take-off, Woitke ordered to us to release our auxiliary fuel tanks as enemy aircraft were in the area and, to be able to escape them, we had to lighten our load. The encounter was not long in coming. Woitke's aircraft was hit by a full burst and was transformed into a ball of fire. Shortly after the explosion, I shot down a Spitfire in a circling combat; one of my comrades confirmed the victory over the radio. I was the only pilot of our formation to get back to Rheine safe and sound. In accordance with instructions, I made out a combat report which was sent, as usual, to the *Kommodore*. In the evening, I was called to the telephone: '*The Kommodore wants to speak to you!*' I waited for his congratulations on my victory. This was not to be the case. On the contrary, I received a telling-off, which made me angry. In effect, I was the only pilot of the *Gruppe* to release the fuel tank just after take-off. Because of this, it made it impossible for me to become involved in lengthy combat and I returned to base far earlier than my comrades. He announced his intention to place me before a court-martial for cowardice in the face of the enemy. I argued vehemently against these accusations, gave him a piece of my mind concerning my honour, and slammed the phone down. I was beside myself with anger. My fellow officers intervened on my behalf, and later, the *Kommodore* appeared to have completely forgotten about our telephone conversation. On the following day, 25 December, it was sunny, but cold. I was shot down (my fifth time) by a Spitfire and had to bale out."

There was no rest on Christmas Day. Nearly 400 B-17s and B-24s carried out raids on communications centres in western Germany. All three *Gruppen* were in action, with I. *Gruppe* particularly successful; seven Liberators were shot down by *Lt.* Demuth, *Hptm.* Ehlers and *Lt.* Just among the claimants. However, the price paid for these victories was high, III. *Gruppe* suffering the heaviest losses with four pilots killed, including *Oblt.* Fritz Bilfinger, *Staffelkapitän* of 10. *Staffel*, and two wounded. A complete *Schwarm* from 10./JG 1 led by *Ofw.* Friedrich Zander did not return. Zander was killed a short time after having claimed his *Gruppe's* only *Abschuss* of the day, a P-51 (his 37th claim).

Lt. Rudolf Schnappauf, a very experienced I.*Gruppe* pilot and former wingman to Walter Oesau, was reported missing in action after having claimed his third victory, a P-51. He would be found in the wreckage of his Fw 190 A-8 a week later, on 1 January 1945.

There was no respite on 26 December and eight pilots went missing, including three of the more experienced pilots of II. *Gruppe*, *Lt.* Horst Ertmann, *Ofw.* Georg Hutter and *Ofw.* Reinhard

Fw. Hans-Georg Sperling in front of Bf 109 G-10s or G-14/As of III./JG 1 at Anklam in late Autumn 1944. He was wounded on 25 December during combat with B-17s.

LEFT: *Hptm. Harald Moldenauer (right) replaced Hptm. Erich Woitke who was killed on 24 December 1944, as Kommandeur of III./JG 1. To the left is Oblt. Hans-Joachim Janke, Staffelkapitän of 11./JG 1.*

RIGHT AND FAR RIGHT: Over a cup of coffee, Hptm. Hans Ehlers, Gruppenkommandeur of I./JG 1 and his Kommodore, Herbert Ihlefeld (right), plot the course of an enemy bomber incursion.

Hptm. Hans Ehlers, Kommandeur of II./JG 1, who had a tough reputation among his men, was killed in action on 27 December 1944.

RIGHT: JG 1 lost many experienced pilots at the end of 1944, such as Lt. Otto Bach (right) who was killed 26 November 1944 and Ofw. Georg Hutter (left), killed on 26 December 1944, both from II./JG 1.

Flecks. The following day, it was the turn of I. *Gruppe* to suffer. At 10.15 hrs, *Hptm*. Hans Ehlers led 18 Fw 190s on a mission to cover troops in the Dinant-Rochefort area. They were challenged to the west of Mayen by a flight of Mustangs from the 364th Fighter Group and lost six pilots killed. Among the dead were *Lt*. Gottfried Just, *Staffelkapitän* of 2. *Staffel*, *Lt*. Richard Förster who succeeded the malaria-stricken *Lt*. Hanf as head of 4./JG 1 and *Gruppenkommandeur* Hans Ehlers, shot down in his Fw 190 A-8, 'White 20'. At the time of his death, Ehlers had 52 victories, including 20 four-engined bombers. His final tally was probably higher, but details of his successes during the Normandy campaign were never brought officially to account. Ehlers was a respected figure among his men and the *Gruppe* never quite got over his loss. Set against this disaster were claims for six P-51s by I. *Gruppe*, including one by *Lt*. Demuth of 3./JG 1 and two by *Lt*. Luepke.

Demuth remembered: "On 27 December, we took off for one of those murderous missions over the Ardennes. I noticed a large formation of Mustangs which approached us from the rear. I shouted clearly over the radio: *'Ehlers, from Demuth. Watch out, Mustang behind us! Turn!'* Ehlers answered me: *'Shut up, Demuth, we have orders to do a strafing run; and an order is an order!'* They were to be Ehlers' last words. Victorious in so many missions, he became easy prey for the American hunters, just like *Lt*. Just and some of the others."

Oberfähnrich Gerhard Stiemer of 3./JG 1: "On 25 December, *Oblt*. Pörsch, *Uffz*. Toni Riemer and myself took off together with some Fw 190 D-9s to Twente. During the journey, we saw two British fighters, but we did not try to take them on. While landing, *Oblt*. Pörsch damaged his aircraft. Next day, 26 Fw 190 A-8s from our *Gruppe* took off from Twente for Bastogne on an infantry support mission. Our formation reached the area without meeting the enemy. Nevertheless, radio contact with the ground was difficult and it was extremely hard to recognise our objectives since the front line was not really visible. We returned without success after having been fired at by AA guns. Shortly after having crossed the frontier, we received the order to land in Bad Lippspringe and Paderborn. The latter field, being further away, was hardly a logical option because we didn't have enough fuel. Some pilots just made it and several made wheels-up landings on their last drops. Led away by *Hptm*. Ehlers, the remainder of *Gruppe* landed at Bad Lippspringe. On the 27th, we received the order to carry out a new mission in the Dinant area. Ehlers's unit joined us above Paderborn. Its Fw 190s carried auxiliary tanks, while ours, having started from Paderborn, did not. Some Bf 109s from JG 3 *Udet* provided us with an escort as far as Köln. Then, *Hptm*. Ehlers split the *Gruppe* into individual *Schwärme* before going down to low level. In the clear weather, we spotted some P-38s, P-47s and P-51s flying at different heights above us. As they did not seem to notice us, Ehlers ordered us to continue with the mission. After about ten minutes, the last *Schwarm* signalled that some P-51s were turning in order to get into attack position. At such a low altitude, our formation did not have a chance against the Mustangs and the *Schwärme* were shot down one by one. Ehlers remained imperturbable despite these catastrophic events. *'Go on! Get them!'* he cried into the radio. To my right, *Fw.* Oswald's aircraft exploded. Almost simultaneously, my tail was hit and my aircraft was shaken by an explosion. I turned immediately to the left. A P-51 pursued me, but its superior speed made him pass under me before making a large turn. He appeared some moments later in my *Revi*. I opened fire immediately and hit him. Now, I was so low that I could have touched the top of the trees. Then an aircraft which I could not identify appeared in front of me. We opened fire at each other simultaneously. My engine was hit and oil spattered across my windscreen. The airspeed indicator fell to zero. A hill appeared in front of me. I tried to gain some altitude and lost consciousness at that moment. I woke up lying on a sofa in a farmhouse at Todenfeld, near Rheinbach, with a military doctor at my side. Apparently, a *Panzer* crew had extracted me from the wreckage of my heavily damaged aircraft which had come down in the farmhouse's garden. It had been hit in the tail, the cockpit, and the fuselage. Two cylinders as well as a prop blade were missing. The *Panzer* crew had witnessed the last moments of another Fw 190 above Todenfeld. It must have been my comrade, Förster, who was shot down by a pair of Mustangs."

Lt. Hans Berger, the *Staffelkapitän* of 3./JG 1 offers a revealing and honest insight into one aspect of conditions within a *Luftwaffe* fighter unit at this time: "At the end of 1944, I returned to I./JG 1, the unit which I had left following the fighting over the Invasion Front. By now, everything had changed. Most of my comrades had disappeared; some had been posted to other units, but the great majority had been killed in action. I could feel that the mood had changed. The fact that we, the officers, were quartered separately from the soldiers had become normal since our departure from Schiphol, and certainly did nothing to strengthen the link between the men in the *Staffel*; but now a deep fracture appeared in the Officer Corps itself. The attitudes adopted by each of us when so close to death are radically different. I believe that this behaviour can be created by individuals belonging to different social classes. While, in peacetime, to become an officer required high quality attributes, in time of war, several brave soldiers were promoted to higher rank due only to their courage in battle. So, several fighter *Gruppen* were placed under the command of good pilots but very poor leaders. These men were often unable to psychologically handle the extremely difficult situation in which we fought, to assume their authority in a skilful manner, and above all, to help their men avoid unnecessary losses in action. On the contrary, often chasing after awards and promotion, the only important thing for them was to claim the maximum of victories, even if the cost was high in wingmen or inexperienced pilots. Discovering their incapacity in their role, these wartime officers often used a blind authoritarianism, and many of them were alcoholics. I saw them nearly daily drinking in officers' messes. Some drank an entire bottle of Cognac every day. When some young *Leutnante*, such as me, refused to drink in such an ill-considered manner, I had to withstand constant taunting. Many of the German aces, about whom one hears so much, were not, in truth, such good examples of leadership."

ABOVE: *Lt.* Gottfried Just seen seated in the cockpit of his Fw 190 A-8 'Black 9' as the Staffel prepare for take-off. Just was killed in action on 27 December 1944.

BELOW: On 27 December 1944, I./JG 1 suffered heavy casualties in the Eifel. Wounded, *Ofhr.* Gerhard Stiemer, managed to belly-land his Fw 190 A-8 (W.Nr.739274) in a garden at Todenfeld.

270 JG 1 – Defenders of the Reich

In September 1944, I./JG 1 was based at Eggebek near Husum where it re-built its strength and repleted its ranks with young, freshly trained pilots. One training flight ended with the port undercarriage leg of Fw 190 A-8 'Yellow 8' (W.Nr.171596) collapsing with Ofhr. Hans Caris at the controls. This aircraft was normally flown by Lt. Hans Berger.

Focke-Wulf Fw 190 A-8 W.Nr.171596 'Yellow 8'
Ofhr. Hans Caris,
I./JG 1
Eggebek
September 1944

A Bf 109 G-6/AS of III./JG 1 at Anklam, late Autumn 1944. The Geschwader emblem on the engine cowling and the red band on the rear fuselage is clearly visible on the light blue overall colour scheme.

Messerschmitt Bf 109 G-6/AS
III./JG 1
Anklam
late Autumn 1944

LEFT: *Pilots of I./JG 1 in front of a Fw 190 A-8 at Greifswald, late November 1944.*
From left to right: Fhr. Schreck, Lt. Just, Lt. Neuner, Ofhr. Hostermann and to the far right, Uffz. Schaumburg.

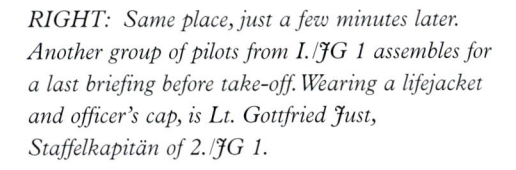

RIGHT: *Same place, just a few minutes later. Another group of pilots from I./JG 1 assembles for a last briefing before take-off. Wearing a lifejacket and officer's cap, is Lt. Gottfried Just, Staffelkapitän of 2./JG 1.*

272 JG 1 – Defenders of the Reich

**Messerschmitt Bf 109 G-6
reportedly flown by Obstlt. Herbert Ihlefeld,
Geschwaderkommodore
JG 1,
Gruhno
Autumn 1944**

*According to an unconfirmed source,
Obstlt. Herbert Ihlefeld, Kommodore of JG 1,
made an emergency landing in a field near
Gruhno in the Autumn of 1944 in this aircraft.
Clearly seen is the red fuselage band as well as an
unusual double chevron forward of the
Balkenkreuz. Examination of the photographs
reveals considerable retouching of the machine's
paintwork.*

RIGHT: This view, and the ones which follow show pilots of JG 1 at readiness at Greifswald, November 1944.

LEFT: Pilots of 4./JG 1; from left: Uffz. Brand, Uffz. Riemer, Uffz. Mietling (back), Fhr. Schlarb, Fhr. Köttgen, Uffz. Rechenbach, Lt. Förster and Uffz. Fritzsche.

*BELOW: Some of these pilots from I./JG 1 are recognizable; from right: Uffz. Fritzsche, Fhr. Köttgen, hidden, Uffz. Riemer, Fhr. Schlarb.
Third from left: Uffz. Brand.*

THIS PAGE AND OPPOSITE: Following their waiting at readiness, pilots assemble and commence take-off, the Stab starting first, followed respectively by 3., 2., 1. and 4./JG 1. Note the dark late-war Balkenkreuzen of the Fw 190 A-8s, some of which have rounded canopies, the Kettenkrad towing the Anlasswagen, as well as the wearing of yellow arm bands to denote 'Deutsche Luftwaffe', so as to avoid German pilots being mistaken for Allied airmen. Civilians were known to lynch captured enemy airmen.

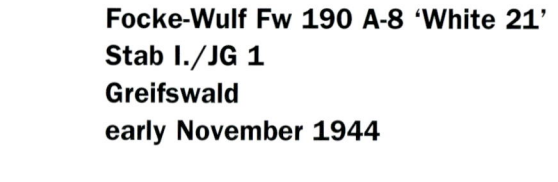

Focke-Wulf Fw 190 A-8 'White 21'
Stab I./JG 1
Greifswald
early November 1944

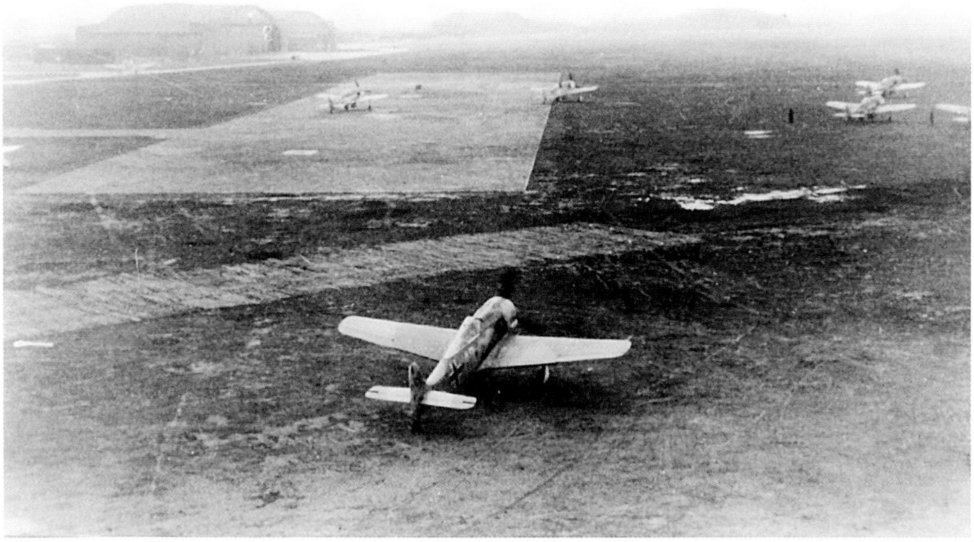

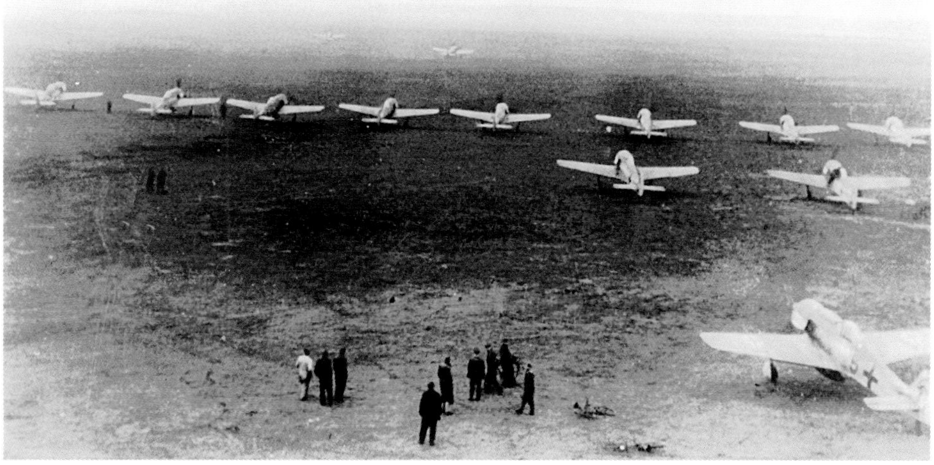

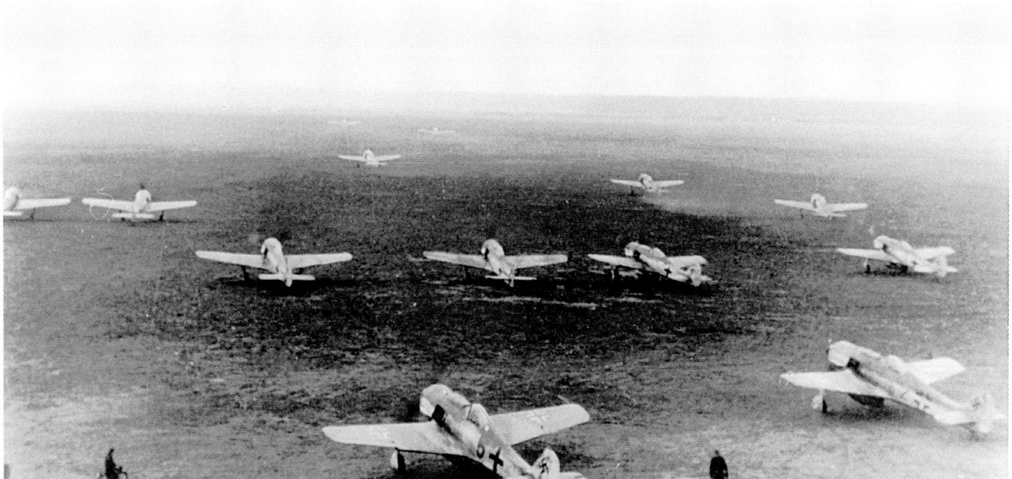

276 JG 1 – Defenders of the Reich

Three Fw 190 A-8s of 2./JG 1 at Greifswald, November 1944. The lack of red fuselage bands indicates that this photograph was taken some time after their delivery.

Focke-Wulf Fw 190 A-8 W.Nr. 173943 'Black 12'
2./JG 1
Greifswald
early November 1944

Fw 190 A-8 'Black 12' (W.Nr. 173943) of 2./JG 1 at Greifswald, early November 1944. The aircraft is fitted with the usual additional 115 ltr drop tank attached with an ETC 501 rack. The fuselage carries a red Defence of the Reich band. Note the glossy paint on the drop tank. Handed over to II./JG 1, this aircraft was 25 per cent damaged on 11 March 1945.

Focke-Wulf Fw 190 A-8 'Black 2'
I./JG 1
Greifswald
early November 1944

ABOVE: Detail of white spiral marking on the front of propeller.

ABOVE: Seated in his Fw 190 A-8, a pilot of I./JG 1 is assisted by his 1st Wart standing on the wing.

RIGHT: Fw 190 A-8s of I./JG 1 at Greifswald. Note in the foreground the Kettenkrad which has just towed an 'Anlasswagen' to Fw 190 W.Nr. 173943, as well as the white markings on the blades of one of the aircraft.

An line-up of Fw 190 A-8s of I./JG 1 at Greifswald, early November 1944.
The Staffel is probably 3./JG 1 since the aircraft in the foreground carries a roughly applied 'Yellow 2'. Note the rounded canopy (characteristic of an Fw 190 A-9) as well as the late-style Balkenkreuz.

Focke-Wulf Fw 190 A-8 'Yellow 2'
probably 3./JG 1
Greifswald
early November 1944

Pilots of I./JG 1 at Greifswald, November-December 1944. Known pilots include from left to right: Fw. Kilian, Lt. Birnbaum, Lt. Luepke (open jacket), Uffz. Stenschke, Ofw. Treptau, Fhr. Schreck, Uffz. Eck, Fhr. Caris, Lt. Just (on motorcycle), Uffz. Riemer, Lt. Stiemer, Uffz. Hostermann. In the background, Fw 190 A-8 'White 23' of Stab I./JG 1 with a late-war 'empty' Balkenkreuz.

Focke-Wulf Fw 190 A-8 'White 23'
Stab I./JG 1
Greifswald
November-December 1944

Focke-Wulf Fw 190 A-8 'Yellow 8'
Ofhr. Gerhard Stiemer
3./JG 1
Greifswald
December 1944

LEFT: On 17 December 1944, I./JG 1 was transferred from Greifswald to Twente. During this flight, Ofhr. Gerhard Stiemer, of 3./JG 1, experienced engine problems in his Fw 190 A-8 'Yellow 8'. He made a wheels-up landing near Celle.

RIGHT: Fw 190 A-8 'Red 3' of 4./JG 1 (W.Nr. 960553). Transferred to 2./JG 1, this aircraft was subsequently re-numbered 'Black 9' and was flown by Staffelführer Gottfried Just when he was shot down and killed on 27 December 1944.

Focke-Wulf Fw 190 A-8 W.Nr. 960553 'Red 3'
4./JG 1
November-December 1944

Chapter Twenty-One

'Bodenplatte'

"On that day, at around 09.00 hrs, I left my house in the Ledeberg quarter in order to take New Year wishes to my family. The weather was cold but beautiful. Soon, I heard the noises of battle above me and I saw a German aircraft flying very low and slow and also firing its guns. I also spotted an English one which was flying very fast. I could see the German aircraft flying alongside the Hundelgem Steenweg as if it was about to land or as if the pilot was hit. Then, still flying very slowly, he slightly turned towards the left and went out of my sight. Thus, I had the time to see the swastika and a red band marking. About one hour later, I heard that a German aircraft had crashed in Elisabethlaan and I ran to see it. It had come down in a flower shop and a great part of the aircraft was to be seen embedded in the first floor. The pilot's body was lying in the street, blackened and mutilated. Nobody bothered about it. During the afternoon, I went back to the site and, to my astonishment, saw that the body was still there."

(Fourteen year-old Louis Volleman, resident of Gent).

January 1945

Hptm. Hans Ehlers' successor was *Hptm.* Georg Hackbarth, who had joined JG 1 on 1 November 1944. Formerly with II./JG 51, he had accumulated 13 victories to his credit. Shortly after his appointment, Hackbarth was informed of the major *Luftwaffe* fighter effort, codenamed Operation *Bodenplatte*.

The OKL were aware of the inability of the *Jagdwaffe* to carry out its intended tasks. It was now more depleted than ever and it was recognised that the few experienced pilots left could not shoulder the entire burden of combat operations. The Ardennes offensive appeared lost. With improved weather conditions, the Allied air forces were able to provide the necessary support that their ground troops needed, and the *Luftwaffe* was incapable of stopping it. A plan, in preparation since mid-December, envisaged a mass, surprise strike against key Allied airfields across Holland, Belgium and France. The tactical belief behind the operation was that if the *Luftwaffe* was not able to wrest control of the skies from the Allies in the air, perhaps it could destroy them on the ground.

Generalmajor Dietrich Peltz, an accomplished former bomber 'ace' and *Ritterkreuzträger* who now commanded II. *Jagdkorps,* was the originator of the idea and he and his staff waited for favourable weather conditions before committing an estimated 1,000 German fighters to the attack. The meteorological forecast pointed to 1 January as being the best day for the operation. The commanders of the assigned fighter units were called together, with senior staff officers communicating to them the still secret details of the plan. On returning to their airfields, they informed their pilots. Any New Year's Eve celebrations were ruled out.

Uffz. August Michalski was a member of the groundcrew with 1./JG 1: "On 31 December, just before nightfall, our chief came into our quarters, located some six or seven kilometres from the airfield, and told us to get to work. All the aircraft had to be ready for flying by 05.00 in the morning. The Fw 190 which I was working on had serious damage in the oil sump. We worked without a break in the freezing cold. At 03.00, the aircraft were finally ready."

Oblt. Fritz Wegner of 5./JG 1 recalled: "To understand what happened to our II. *Gruppe* during the operation, it is necessary to look back one week. On Christmas Day, my *Gruppe* had been involved in a major combat with Mustangs and Thunderbolts. Like a lot of our pilots, I was shot down and had to bale out. I reached my base again at nine o'clock on the morning of 26 December. The *Gruppe* had already received the order to mount an attack on the Bastogne area. *Hauptmann* Staiger and other pilots were already in their machines, and they took off without me. Arriving at the objective, a murderous combat ensued, in which nearly all of our pilots were shot down. One of the few to escape was the *Gruppenkommandeur,* Staiger. Badly shocked, he had to land near Frankfurt, some distance from our airfield. He was therefore not present for the *Bodenplatte* attack. The strength of the *Gruppe* was further diluted by this blood bath. I had to fill the gaps by retaining with II. *Gruppe* the 15 ferry pilots who had brought us some fresh Fw 190s. Among these men were experienced pilots, retired from active service following injuries, but who had never flown these types of mission before. I kept them, however. On the morning of 31 December, I was called to Fürstenau by the High Command, where I was appraised of the plan of attack for the following day. In the evening, having returned to our base at Drope, I called the pilots together and, swearing them to secrecy, outlined the plan of the operation."

1 January: at Twente, Drope and Rheine, the respective airfields of JG 1's three component *Gruppen*, the pilots were roused from their unsettled sleep shortly before 06.00 hrs. Their

commanders went over the plans for the mission for the last time. I. and III. *Gruppen* would attack the Belgian airfield of Maldegem, 15 km (9 mls) to the east of Brugge while II. *Gruppe* would hit the airfield of St. Denijs-Westrem. *Oblt.* Hans-Gottfried Meinhof's 4. *Staffel* was to attack the small airfield of Ursel midway between Gent and Maldegem. Meinhof was a former reconnaissance pilot recently appointed *Staffelführer*.

At 08.10 hrs at Twente, two Ju 88 G night-fighters took off for the west. They were to be the pathfinders for the single-engined fighters. The 20 Fw 190 A-8s flew only 50 m (164 ft) above the ground. Behind them, 30 small black dots gathered in the grey, morning sky. These were the Bf 109 G-14s of III. *Gruppe*, which had taken off from Rheine at 08.15 hrs. The two formations joined up. Everything seemed to be going perfectly. But as the German formation approached Den Haag, the situation changed dramatically. The *Flak* batteries had not been advised of the fighters' course and, without their FuG 25 sets, the fighters were not able to contact them. The batteries opened fire with murderous precision. Four aircraft were hit, including Herbert Ihlefeld's aircraft. The *Geschwaderkommodore* had to make a forced landing. The three other pilots were killed.

Managing to avoid this obstacle, I. and III. *Gruppen* flew over the chill waters of the North Sea. They followed the Belgian coast and then set course south, for a point between Knokke and Blankenberge. They were only a few minutes away from their objective.

At Drope, at around 08.15 hrs, a green flare hissed into the sky and cleared the 30 Fw 190 A-8s of II. *Gruppe* for take-off. Their course was similar to that of their comrades in the other *Gruppen*. They too flew over the German *Flak* batteries, which again opened fire. Over the sea, the *Gruppe* changed course towards Gent. The pilots could now see the aircraft of I. and III. *Gruppen*.

Arriving over Bruges, *Oblt.* Meinhof and his four pilots broke away from the rest of the formation as pre-arranged and headed for the Allied airfield at Ursel. They made several passes and set alight a B-17 undergoing repair, a Mosquito and two Lancasters. The damage to aircraft would have been greater had not the majority of Spitfires based there returned to England the previous day.

I. and III. *Gruppen*, overtaken by II. *Gruppe*, also split up; some aircraft, including that flown by *Gruppenkommandeur* Hackbarth, launched an attack on St. Denijs-Westrem, whilst others attacked Maldegem, where there was total confusion. The airfield lacked anti-aircraft defences, which had been withdrawn a few days earlier. Coming in at tree-top height, the German aircraft had trouble finding their targets; the Spitfires had been dispersed well, and the dense smoke from a burning tank partly obscured the airfield. Towards 09.30 hrs, the German fighters left, leaving the smoking wrecks of 12 Spitfires of 485 (New Zealand) Squadron behind them, as well as a further two damaged. 485 Squadron lost three-quarters of its aircraft.

II. *Gruppe*, together with some aircraft from I. *Gruppe* which had formated with them, appeared over St. Denijs-Westrem, the home of 131 (Polish) Wing. Spitfires from 302, 308 and 317 Squadrons had taken off at about the same time as the German pilots to carry out attacks in the Woensdrecht area. As the Focke-Wulfs arrived, so also did 302 Squadron, which had just returned from its mission and were in the course of landing. F/O Chojnacki of 308 Squadron, who was flying with 302 Squadron, closed quickly on the German aircraft and engaged them. He shot down an Fw 190, probably flown by *Fw.* Karl Hahn and which crashed into a building on the airfield and finished up on top of a Flying Fortress. Seconds later, chased by three German aircraft, Chojnacki was shot down and killed.

Uffz. Gerhard Behrens of 8./JG 1 was one of the numerous victims of the Bodenplatte operation. He was killed in the Gent area.

Fw 190 A-8 'Red 1' (W.Nr. 739269) flown by Uffz. Alfred Fritzsche of 4./JG 1 and captured on 1 January 1945 at De Pinte, near Gent.

The German pilots were strafing the airfield when Flight Sergeant Josef Stanowky of 308 Squadron appeared. Though short of fuel, he followed the other aircraft of his squadron. Sighting the Fw 190s, he shot two down, one to the south of Gent, the other in the centre of town (probably *Hptm.* Hans Georg Hackbarth). The Polish pilot then made a wheels-up landing. The rest of 308 Squadron, having successfully tussled with other Fw 190s a few minutes earlier near Lokeren, headed for their airfield. The Polish pilots caught the Germans unawares, and claimed five shot down (one German pilot baled out). One Spitfire was hit and made a wheels-up landing.

The battle continued and 317 Squadron, called back to help, attacked the enemy. It claimed six Fw 190s shot down for the loss of one Spitfire. After 15 minutes of bitter air fighting, the signal to retire was given and the Fw 190s headed east into the sun. They left behind six wrecked Spitfires of 302 Squadron, plus seven shot down or damaged in aerial combat; *Lt.* Hans Berger and *Oblt.* Fritz Wegner were among the claimants. At St. Denijs-Westrem, 85 GCS also lost a Mosquito, four Avro Ansons, one Spitfire and two Auster; a Short Stirling was also lost.

The wreckage of the Fw 190 A-8 of Uffz. Gerhard Behrens of 8./JG 1, 'Blue 14', shot down near Gent on 1 January 1945.

However, Uffz. Gerhard Behrens of 8./JG 1 was among the *Geschwader's* losses. He had observed a lone Spitfire and decided to attack it and, in doing so, left his 'formation' – in effect his *Rotte*, since there was no longer any well-structured German formation. As he followed the Spitfire, he was unaware of another enemy aircraft on his back. The Polish pilot, Tadeusz Szlenkier, fired at Behrens' aircraft and hit its right wing. Losing control, Behrens decided to jump with his parachute, but he did not have sufficient height and was too low to enable the chute to open. For a few moments, civilians on the ground in St Denijs watched as the German pilot 'followed' the curved dive of his stricken aircraft. He hit the ground some 50 metres from his Fw 190. Arriving at the crash site, the civilians were unable to approach the aircraft while its ammunition was still exploding, but they could see Behrens' body lying 150 m from a main road. His head was badly injured. His aircraft was eventually looted.

Some time later, Polish soldiers removed the body but left the wreck of the aircraft so that the victorious Szlenkier could pose beside his victim.

Another German casualty was *Fw.* Fritz Hoffmann of 3./JG 1. He was more fortunate, surviving unhurt having baled out. Once on the ground however, he was captured by civilians. He was forced to surrender his pistol, but attempted to conceal his pilot's knife. However the knife was eventually discovered by one of the civilians and Hoffmann was beaten severely.

Hptm. Georg Hackbarth's Fw 190 crashed into a flower shop near the Saint Pierre railway station in Gent. Fortunately, the shop was closed at the time (the owners were apparently in church). Firemen arrived at the scene quickly and found Hackbarth's body still in the aircraft.

Following his successful wheels-up landing in De Pinte, *Uffz.* Alfred Fritzsche left his aircraft and ran to the cover of a nearby wood. A day-long search was mounted to find the German pilot before he was found and captured.

The return flight was troublesome; *Oblt.* Meinhof was hit and crashed to his death near Breda. Upon return, at about 10.40 hrs, the news was bad; 17 pilots had been killed, including *Hptm.* Hackbarth and the Latvian pilot, *Fw.* Harrijs Klints, and six pilots were assumed to have been taken as prisoners of war. However, Fw. Klints was, in fact, buried a few metres from his crashed aircraft at Zwijnaarde, but without any official grave, the pilot is still listed as missing.

The hardest hit unit was 5. *Staffel*, which reported five pilots missing including its Austrian *Kapitän, Lt.* Ernst von Johannides.

Following the catastrophic losses suffered over the previous two months culminating in *Bodenplatte*, the *Jagdwaffe* played only a minor role in the future strategy of the German war effort. A total of 151 pilots was reported killed or missing as a result of the raid on 1 January, including three *Geschwaderkommodore*, six *Gruppenkommandeure* and ten *Staffelkapitäne*. The young pilots still in action at the end of the year were the lucky ones. But even amongst these survivors, depth of experience was rare. The shortage of experienced officers in I. *Gruppe* was evident. *Hptm.* Hackbarth had led the *Gruppe* for only five days when he fell in combat on 1 January. Officially, the responsibility for leading the *Gruppe* in the air fell once again to *Lt.* Emil Demuth, but on 3 January, *Major* Günther Capito, a former bomber pilot, assigned to take over I./JG 1, arrived at Twente.

Capito remembers: "During the night of 3-4 January, following a bad train journey, I presented myself before *Oberstleutnant* Ihlefeld. He appointed me to the leadership of I. *Gruppe*, but immediately stated one condition; in the air, the chief of 3. *Staffel*, *Lt*. Demuth, was to lead the *Gruppe*. This restriction to my duties was made with the best of intentions for I lacked experience of both being a fighter pilot as well as leading a *Gruppe*. During the early days, fresh young pilots arrived from the training schools, together with new machines. Around 11 January, we were back up to strength again, although experience was cruelly lacking. We carried out our first formation flight under Demuth's direction. I flew as Number 6."

"On the 12th, following the Russian offensive and the establishment of the bridgehead at Baranow, we were ordered to leave for the East. The *Kommodore* left the same evening to discuss matters with his superiors. We were due to leave on the morning of the 14th, but an intense fog enveloped the region so that a take-off with 'green' pilots was too dangerous. A message arrived; a large formation of 'Indians' was reported over the North Sea. Towards 09.00 the mist lifted slightly and I gave the order to take off. Following the *Stabsschwarm*, I saw one *Staffel* airborne while the three others were lining up to take off. We flew for less than 15 minutes at 50 m (164 ft) altitude when we hit a blanket of fog. Over the radio I heard Demuth's voice: *'Airfield beneath us, everybody land.'* Not seeing it, I ordered the pilots to carry on. I had great experience of blind flying and could evaluate such a danger very accurately. *'Rabe 6' ('Raven 6') here, don't land; climb and reassemble around the machine waggling its wings.'* I repeated this order several times. Five machines joined me and we landed at Fassberg without problem. The others were lost from sight. Arriving at Werneuchen in the afternoon, I finally received information about my men; the *Stabsschwarm* and two *Staffeln* had, in effect, taken off with us. Now our pilots were completely scattered over the whole of northern Germany, from Hamburg to Brandenburg-Briest. It was on this airfield that Demuth and two other pilots had landed. I was also advised of the loss of two or three aircraft. More seriously, 1. and 2. *Staffeln* were not able to leave at the same time as us, as the fog suddenly came down and prevented them from joining us. After 15 minutes the two *Staffeln* were finally able to take off. The 'Indians' arrived at that precise moment…"

Twente – 09.15 hrs. The delayed Focke-Wulfs started their take-off routine. At that moment Spitfires of the RAF's Second Tactical Air Force swooped out of the sky. The German pilots were completely taken by surprise. Eleven smoking craters pocked the airfield. Lack of height meant that the German pilots were unable to bale out. Two Spitfires were shot down, including one by *Uffz*. Sill. Sill from the *Stab*. I./JG 1, was killed shortly after his victory. He was flying a 'long-nosed' Fw 190 D-9, one of the few aircraft of this type recently delivered to the *Geschwaderstab* and *Gruppenstab* of I. *Gruppe*. *Oblt*. Heinrich Greuner, Meinhof's successor as head of 4./JG 1, survived the attack but lost his life an hour later crashing with his aircraft.

Major Capito: "… Ihlefeld threatened me with arrest and court-martial. I avoided having to present myself before him on the airfield at Königsberg due to a transfer which had been arranged for me three days before. The threats were dropped and I learned later that the I. *Gruppe* pilots were able to reassemble on 15 January at Werneuchen, from where they reached their destination."

Uffz. Alvo von Alvensleben of 1. *Staffel*, recently arrived at the unit, completes the story: "On 14 January, I was delayed by my Fw 190 suffering from mechanical trouble. At 08.00, I reported to my *Staffelkapitän* and rejoined my friend, *Unteroffizier* Heidrich, to help him finish his preparations. The *Schwärme*, four aircraft wing-tip to wing-tip, from all *Staffeln* began to move on the airfield. The first aircraft took off and disappeared beyond the horizon. During this succession of take-offs, just as Heidrich's *Schwarm* reached take-off speed and left the ground, about ten Spitfires emerged from the clouds and closed in on the German aircraft. The Spitfires' cannon opened up, followed by German MGs replying. While I was taking shelter, I saw several Fw 190s crash and explode. My friend was among them. There was nothing more to say about the engagement. Remaining alone at Twente, I was not able to take off and rejoin my unit at Heiligenbeil until 1 February, in view of the intense enemy air activity."

Uffz. Heinz Lehmann of 9./JG 1 photographed in his Bf 109 'White 9' at Rheine shortly before the Staffel was posted to the East. Note the 'Erla-Haube' cockpit.

Chapter Twenty-Two

JG 1 in the East

On 16 January 1945, two trains left Holland and headed east. They carried the ground personnel of I./JG 1, as well as all the necessary equipment required at the unit's new base on the Eastern Front. The German military situation in the East was deteriorating fast. The Soviet armed forces could count on 6,000,000 men and women, the *Reich* half that number. In material terms, German strength was about one fifth of that of the Soviets. The Red Army was fighting in the streets of Budapest and it had reopened its offensive in central Poland. In all, 180 Soviet divisions were in action; the Germans could only call upon 75. On the northern front, Army Group North and other forces had been isolated in Kurland since mid-October 1944 and it would be Kurland which would be JG 1's new theatre of operations. After a journey of four days, the first train arrived at Jürgenfelde, near Insterburg. Immediately coming under Russian fire, it had to pull back. The second train was diverted to Heiligenbeil, where the pilots who had evacuated Jürgenfelde were awaited. Heiligenbeil was reached at 16.00 hrs on 22 January. A new transfer order arrived because the Russians continued to break through. At Heiligenbeil large numbers of refugees streamed westwards, trying to stay ahead of the Red Army which was rolling up everything before it. Four field kitchens belonging to I. *Gruppe* arrived in the nick of time.

On 24 January, a move by rail to Königsberg was possible, but two days later the train had to be abandoned, and some personnel managed to reach an airfield near Neukuhren. At minus 22 degrees centigrade, the weather was bitter.

On 30 January, fresh information arrived to the effect that the Russians were barely 20 km (12 mls) away. After further moves, at 22.30 hrs on 4 February, the column, numbering 65 wagons, finally arrived at Rahmel airfield, near Danzig, where it was once again at the disposal of the *Gruppenkommandeur* and the flying personnel. The men were not to know that a further transfer order awaited them the following day. But what happened to JG 1 was just one example of what was happening across the ever-shrinking German-held territory. Nearly every unit moving from west to east encountered similar difficulties.

The worries of the pilots moving east were of a completely different order. Their duties were to escort maritime convoys in the Baltic Sea, the only hope for troops and civilians encircled in the Kurland pocket. These pilots knew that they were up against not just Russian tanks, but also anti-aircraft batteries as renowned as their own.

After its disastrous departure from the West in mid-January, I. *Gruppe* could muster only ten pilots. The first five arrived at Jürgenfelde four days later under *Oblt.* Emil Demuth, the recently-appointed Staffelkapitän of 3./JG 1; the rest, led by *Lt.* Luepke, arrived the following day. On 20 January, operations began for these ten pilots when they had to 'clear' the airspace around Insterburg. Two pilots went missing following an engagement with Russian Laggs, with *Fhr.* Richde claiming one of the enemy. Jürgenfelde soon had to be evacuated in the face of the advancing Soviets and a move to Gutenfelde followed on 23 January, then Neukuhren on 26 January, Heiligenbeil later on 26 January and Danzig on 2 February. These continuing changes of base left little time for combat operations which should have taken the form of ground attack sorties and escort to transport aircraft. On 30 January, *Oblt.* Demuth recorded his seventeenth and last victory, a Yak-9.

"Missions on the Eastern Front were difficult to fly because of the weather conditions more than the enemy opposition," Demuth recalls. "Snow covered everything and the mist was always so intense that it was almost impossible to find something on the ground to help orientation. My experience in flight without visibility – experience that I gained on the Stalingrad front two years earlier as a *Transportflieger* evacuating wounded soldiers – was very precious to everyone. As a consequence of these chaotic operations in the east in January-February 1945, I nearly lost eight technicians from my *Gruppe*. Indeed, when the greatest part of our ground personnel evacuated with trucks towards the west, we eight pilots, with our best *Warten*, stayed on at Heiligenbeil in order to get our last eight Fw 190s serviceable. We could already hear the sounds of battle, explosions, Russian tanks and so on, when we were advised by radio that no more Ju 52s would land at Heiligenbeil to pick up our technicians. On 2 February, just after having been ordered to evacuate towards Danzig, I ordered the first aid boxes and radios removed from all the Fw 190s so as to accommodate one technician in each fuselage behind the cockpit. I gave orders to my pilots to avoid combat and we took off. After a short flight, we landed without problem on the icy strip of Danzig. This way, our *Warten* escaped capture by the Russians."

On 7 February, while Demuth and his men were at Garz on the Island of Usedom, a new order reached them; they were to pass their Fw 190 A-8s and A-9s to II. *Gruppe* and head for the Heinkel works at Parchim, 70 km south of Rostock.

For their part, II. *Gruppe* left for the Eastern Front under the control of *Oblt.* Fritz Wegner, *Staffelführer* of 6. *Staffel*. *Major* Hermann Staiger had been given command of one of the *Gruppen* of the Me 262-equipped *Jagdgeschwader* 7. Arriving at Insterburg airfield on 18 January, II./JG 1 immediately went into action. For the first time, pilots encountered Russian Yak-3 and Yak-9 fighters. Two were killed during this first engagement. Meanwhile, returning to Insterburg, it was discovered that the airfield had been bombed to the point where it was impossible to land. The Focke-Wulfs were diverted to Jürgenfelde which was used by I. *Gruppe*. Over the next two days, several further missions were flown in the Insterburg region, resulting in more losses, including *Hptm.* Friedrich Strich, commander of 7. *Staffel*. Bad weather and fog were ever present. Russian tanks continued their advance and retreating pilots carried their first mechanic in the rear of their aircraft. Not being able to evacuate all its aircraft, II. *Gruppe* destroyed ten Fw 190 A-8s and A-9s between 21 and 23 January.

In the air, the escaping aircraft lost their way during the transfer flight, but the majority arrived at Gerdauen, near Königsberg. The retreat continued through Heiligenbeil, Kolberg, Samland and finally Garz/Usedom. On 4 February, the unit was reformed at Garz in order to once again continue operations against Allied four-engined bombers. These now had one objective – Berlin. The defence of the *Luftwaffe's Erprobungsstellen* at Peenemünde and Swinemünde was also assigned to JG 1. Installations at Garz were inadequate with no blast pens. Aircraft had to park along the side of the airstrip. After a week's work, shelters were built and the airfield became operational.

Unteroffizier Konrad Augner of 8./JG 1 recalled: "On 2 January, I was posted as an instructor to *Jagdgeschwader* 106 at Garz. The Russians had reached the Oder and I carried out fighter-bomber missions against pontoons with a 250 kg (551 lb) bomb. The Russians held the important crossroads in the town of Naugart, where five routes crossed and we attacked there also. Shortly after my arrival at Garz, II. *Gruppe*, *Jagdgeschwader* 1 took up quarters there. I was surprised to find among the pilots *Hauptmann* Wolfgang Ludewig, who had been my *Staffelkapitän* when we were both with *Jagdgeschwader* 102 at Zerbst. It was he who, to my great disappointment, arranged my posting as an instructor rather than send me to the front. He advised me that the training units would soon be dissolved, and many of their personnel would be deployed as infantry. As *Staffelkapitän* of 8. *Staffel*, he suggested I became a *Schwarmführer* in his *Staffel*, which led to certain pilots being jealous. During February, we regularly escorted the maritime convoys evacuating those trapped in the Kurland pocket."

"On 25 March, towards 16.00, we were placed on alert. On the previous mission, a pilot had been shot down by our own *Flak* (Author's note: this pilot, *Gefr*. Amandus Strickrock of 6. *Staffel* was killed). We were waiting in the cockpits of our aircraft. The order for take-off was given, but as we moved off, it was cancelled. Four or five minutes later came a further instruction. Take off in four minutes to escort vessels in map-square 'PM' (the Bornholm area). Shortly afterwards – '*Take off, course 60 degrees, height 4,000 metres.*' This course would take us right into the middle of a forbidden zone! The base at Swinemünde was obscured by smoke cover. Not being able to see the smallest ship, we descended, and drew intense fire from the defences. I fired a signal flare and accelerated. I just had time to put another flare in position before I was pulled away from the furnace. A glance to my left, my two comrades were there; to the right – my wingman had disappeared! I looked down, and saw an Fw 190 sinking in the sea. Right over it, I saw a white parachute. I immediately gave *Obergefreiter* Neumann's position to the head of the unit. We had to carry on with the mission. Far from the coast, hunched up in our lifejackets, the sensation was very disagreeable. Finally, we found four long white trails of foam – our ships were there. We moved closer. They were sailing in a north-easterly direction, while those we were due to escort should have been heading to Kurland. It was incomprehensible! A little further on, more trails. A dozen merchant ships of all sizes. In this uncertainty, we flew figures of eight while circling around the two convoys. As we lost altitude, a ship opened fire. We climbed again and continued escort at a safe distance. After an hour it was time to return. We set course 120 degrees and when we saw the chalk cliffs of the nearby Rügen island we knew we were too far to the west, and we therefore headed east. Over Peenemünde, we drew the fire of the anti-aircraft defences once again. Finally, we reached Garz! Shortly after getting out of my Fw 190, a *Kübelwagen* sought me out to take me to HQ, where I made a report of the flight to *Kommodore* Ihlefeld. The following day, a court-martial was arranged in my honour. A map was spread out on the table, and these gentlemen asked me to show our course. I did not and *Hauptmann* Ludewig supported me; it was for them to prove that I had flown over the ships which we were to escort and to which we apparently got too close. I learned later that the ships carried nitro-glycerine, which no doubt explained the nervousness of their gunners. It was a one-off situation."

Uffz. Herbert Neumann was rescued and sent to hospital.

At the end of February, *Major* Staiger's successor, *Hptm*. Paul-Heinrich Dähne, arrived at II. *Gruppe*. Aged 23, Dähne was from Frankfurt-an-der-Oder. He had accumulated 100 victories, gained whilst with JG 52 and JG 11. His arrival coincided with the departure of the *Staffelkapitän* of 6. *Staffel*, *Oblt*. Fritz Wegner, for a training course as a *Gruppenkommandeur*. Wegner spent a month and a half at the *Verbandsführerschule* at Bad Wörishofen. He was then posted to II./JG 300 at Holzkirchen and, on 24 April, he was shot down by *Flak* and wounded. Post-war, he joined the new *Luftwaffe*, and retired in 1981 with the rank of *Generalleutnant*.

Pilots of II./JG 1 at 30 minutes readiness at Garz/Usedom, February-March 1945. Fw. Erwin Steeb is on the left, sitting on fence.

Combat missions undertaken by II. *Gruppe* out of Garz resulted in several losses, among them, on 11 March, *Lt.* Hubert Swoboda, *Staffelkapitän* of 5. *Staffel*. He was found severely wounded and died the same day having parachuted from his aircraft. *Fw.* Erwin Steeb, a pilot of II. *Gruppe* for nearly a year, led 5. *Staffel* during the unit's final operations. *Lt.* Alfred Dürr, who had arrived at the unit at the end of January, became the official *Staffelkapitän*.

Like the other *Gruppen*, III. *Gruppe* was also sent east. Its aircraft left Rheine on 13 January at 14.05 hrs. After a stopover of three days at Straussberg, the unit reached Schröttersburg, 90 km (56 mls) from Varsovia, where two *freie-Jagd* missions were undertaken. During one of them, *Ofw.* Leo-Lothar Barann, who had joined the unit from JG 11 in March 1944, shot down a Il-2, claiming the first Eastern Front victory for his unit and his 23rd personal claim. A move to Thorn resulted in two further missions on the 20th, one a *freie-Jagd*, the other, a ground attack sortie. Thorn was evacuated on 21 and 22 January and after that the *Gruppe* was plunged rapidly into the headlong German retreat. Pilots and essential ground personnel reached Marienburg (Malbork) and from there, on 23 January, Berent (Koscierzyna), south-west of Danzig.

III. *Gruppe* were split up for a short time and its pilots sent to Jesau, Neukuhren and Pillau, where their aircraft were passed on to JG 54. On 31 January, they regrouped at Stolp and received new machines. From this airfield, the unit escorted Fw 190-equipped ground-attack units on tank-busting operations. It also flew escort to the famous *Oberst* Hans-Ulrich Rudel's *Schlachtgeschwader 2 Immelmann*. During these missions, III./JG 1 recorded 12 victories despite suffering fuel shortages. Some believed that the lack of fuel was due to deliberate acts of sabotage.

At the beginning of February, 12 technicians from III. *Gruppe* were trapped when Thorn was encircled. In effect, each time a unit took possession of a base, or when they left, a small detachment arrived in advance, or remained behind. It usually comprised the best mechanics, who would either receive the first machines or who brought the remaining aircraft up to flight-worthy readiness. At Thorn, the rearguard reported to the base commander, who told them the field was to be defended to the last man. The Technical Officer responsible for the technicians maintained radio contact with the unit's headquarters, and they were promised that a Ju 52 would arrive to collect them. To the east of the airfield, as the land battle came closer, Russian tanks could be heard. At midnight, when all hope had just about disappeared, a Ju 52 set down at Thorn and collected the remaining men of the unit.

Uffz. Gerhard Hildenbrand of 11./JG 1 remembers operations at this time: "On 9 February, *Fhr.* Herbert Dönsch, two comrades and myself were released from 11./JG 1 and sent to reinforce 9./JG 1 for a mission to the Dummelsburg area. Landing after the mission, we discovered that Dönsch was missing. Two aircraft from 9./JG 1 immediately took off to look for him. A little later, we saw Dönsch's aircraft approaching at high altitude. The noise of his engine, which was running at too high a pitch, made us think that he had been hit. *Why had he not jumped using his parachute?* Surely, because our strength was so diminished, he wanted to try to save his precious aircraft. Suddenly, he went into a dive, hit the ground and his aircraft exploded near Stolp. On 1 March, I was chosen with three comrades, including *Uffz.* Hermann Völz, for a mission over the front area near Rummelsburg. Völz preceded me at take-off. He left the runway with enough altitude, but his aircraft suddenly lost height by some several metres. My friend nosed up his Bf 109 and just avoided a building to the east of the airfield. But he then crashed into a larger building further on. In spite of the tank full of fuel it carried, the aircraft did not explode. Nevertheless, Hermann was killed, his head smashed against the *Revi* sight."

On 3 and 4 March, III. *Gruppe* left Stolp for Anklam airfield where it had 'rested and refurbished' following the Normandy campaign. It was required to protect the *Erprobungsstellen* at Swinemünde and Peenemünde, and cover the Baltic, from where there poured an ever-growing tide of refugees.

ABOVE: Groundcrew belonging to I./JG 1 arrived at Heiligenbeil on 22 January 1945 and were welcomed by intensely cold weather.

ABOVE: In January 1945, I./JG 1 encountered appalling weather on the Eastern Front. Here groundcrew struggle to haul a Fw 190 out of its woodland dispersal. Note what are possibly yellow streaks on the propeller blades of these Fw 190s, as well as the Balkenkreuz on the wings and the tail Hakenkreuz which have been reduced to dark outlines.

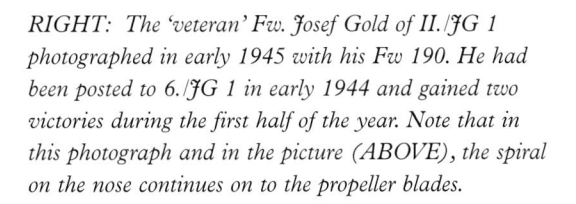

RIGHT: The 'veteran' Fw. Josef Gold of II./JG 1 photographed in early 1945 with his Fw 190. He had been posted to 6./JG 1 in early 1944 and gained two victories during the first half of the year. Note that in this photograph and in the picture (ABOVE), the spiral on the nose continues on to the propeller blades.

ABOVE AND LEFT:
Two Fw 190 A-8s of II./JG 1 under camouflage nets at Garz/Usedom, February 1945.

BELOW: The entire 11./JG 1 pose in front of 'Schönruh' (its operations room) for a photograph at Anklam, March 1945. From left to right:
Uffz. Rozenkranz, Uffz. Eichner, Uffz. Walther, Fhr. Gerold, unknown, Oblt. Janke (Staffelkapitän), Obgfr. Jaap, Ofhr. Hillmer, Obgfr. Juffa, Lt. Sundermeier, Uffz. Welzel, Fw. Hausotter, Uffz. Scholz, Ofw. Haspel, Uffz. Wagner, Uffz. Habig and Uffz. Hildenbrand.

BELOW: Pilots of II./JG 1 at Garz, February-March 1945 with Uffz. Herbert Dosch in the centre.

ABOVE: Pilots of 9./JG 1 line up for a snapshot at Anklam, March 1945. Behind them is Bf 109 'White 5'. Third from left is Fw. Walter Pleines and in the centre, smoking, Staffelführer Oblt. Martin.

ABOVE: Pilots of 9./JG 1 gather for a picture on one of their Bf 109s at Anklam in March 1945. From left: Uffz. Heinrich Esser, Fw. Walter Pleines, Lt. Hubert Heckmann and Uffz. Heinz Lehmann.

ABOVE: Fw. Walter Pleines, Lt. Hubert Heckmann and Uffz. Heinz Lehmann of 9./JG 1 pose for a photograph by a Bf 109 G.

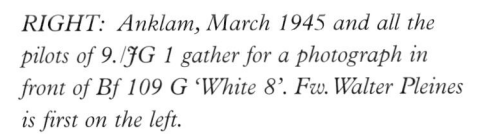

RIGHT: Anklam, March 1945 and all the pilots of 9./JG 1 gather for a photograph in front of Bf 109 G 'White 8'. Fw. Walter Pleines is first on the left.

LEFT: Same place, same time. Gruppenkommandeur Hptm. Harald Moldenhauer (centre) visits the 9. Staffel. In this photograph, Moldenhauer is accompanied by two experienced pilots, Fw. Helmut Fröhlich (left) and Fw. Kurt Baten (right).

LEFT: A Bf 109 G-10/R-3 of 11./JG 1 at Anklam, March 1945, with the unit's operations room in the background.

Lt. Hubert Heckmann of 9./JG 1 at Anklam in March 1945 in his Bf 109 G-10/AS 'White 13'. Shortly after these photographs were taken, Heckmann was transferred to JG 7.

Chapter Twenty-Three

The Peoples' Fighter

February-April 1945

By February 1945, devastated by continual bombing, the Third Reich no longer possessed sufficient quality materials, fuel or experienced pilots with which to maintain any kind of effective air defence. Hitler's Germany had little time left. The research departments worked tirelessly on new projects which might, perhaps, change the course of the war. Strong forces were therefore assigned to protect the test centres such as Peenemünde. On 8 September 1944, the RLM issued a specification requirement for the construction of a fighter capable of reaching 750 km/h (466 mph), yet of such simple build that it could be quickly mass-produced. The aircraft had to be ready before 1 January 1945. The design departments in the various aircraft companies submitted their proposals. Heinkel, who had designed the first jet fighter in 1939, secured the contract. On 30 October, the plans were ready and thousands of workers were mobilised. There was even talk of forming and training a 'Hitler Youth *Luftwaffe*'; the handling characteristics of these small aircraft were such that it was considered that young boys would be able to fly them in combat!

The first prototype of the He 162 *Volksjäger* flew on 6 December 1944 at Vienna-Schwechat, not far from its assembly line. Without doubt, the speed with which it was completed represented an unparalleled feat in the field of aircraft manufacture. Four days later, before a gathering of senior officials, the same aircraft, the He 162 V-1, crashed, taking its test pilot to his death. Heinkel, though conscious of the aircraft's fragility and certain defects and opposed to the test flight, had to see the demonstration through. The dream was over. The reality was that to construct such an aircraft took time. However, despite immense technical problems and wide-scale dispersion of production lines intended to minimise the effect of bombing, the aircraft was put into series production and deliveries to the *Luftwaffe* began towards the end of January 1945. Military tests were conducted on the aircraft by *Erprobungskommando* 162 under the command of *Obstlt.* Heinz Bär, who once again featured in *Jagdgeschwader* 1's history. The test unit was initially based at Rechlin, then at Lechfeld and finally at München-Riem.

In early February 1945, Vienna saw a gathering of those responsible for development of the He 162 project as well as the *General der Jagdflieger*, *Oberst* Gordon Gollob, and his assistant *Oberstleutnant* Walter Dahl. The project finally reached fruition with the creation at Goslar of a new unit, *Jagdgeschwader* 80, which was intended exclusively to fly the He 162. It was also decided to convert *Jagdgeschwader* 1 over to this new aircraft. To this end, on 8 February, I./JG 1 handed over its 23 Fw 190s to II. *Gruppe* and, led by *Oblt.* Emil Demuth, headed for Parchim. In a convoy of 65 wagons, they reached their destination at 02.00 hrs on 9 February. The pilots received theoretical training from technicians and test pilots from the Heinkel-Nord works. 4. *Staffel* was disbanded and its pilots were distributed among the other three *Staffeln* of the *Gruppe*. Eventually joined by the *Geschwaderstab*, I. *Gruppe* spent nearly two months at Parchim.

On 27 February, ten pilots from 2. *Staffel* under *Lt.* Hachtel were sent to Vienna to collect the He 162s arriving off the production lines. The technicians reported that – "*These men were incredibly impatient to take on the He 162s which had been cleared by our technicians. As soon as they were ready, the pilots took over the aircraft.*"

Training began prudently. Nevertheless, on 14 March, *Uffz.* Tautz was killed on his first flight due to pilot error. Furthermore, Hachtel's men returned without aircraft for combat-ready machines were not yet available from the Heidfeld factory.

During the second half of March, ten pilots from I. *Gruppe* were sent briefly to Marienehe near Rostock, another source of He 162s. Still intact, this was the principal Heinkel production works. Lodging in a luxurious hotel at Warnemünde, the pilots took charge of a group of aircraft thoroughly tested by the company's mechanics and test pilots. At the beginning of April, this detachment returned to Parchim where the pilots rejoined the rest of the *Gruppe*, and made their first flights at the end of March. These flights, however, were of between 10 and 20 minutes only.

One of the first and very rare He 162 A-1 Spatz delivered to I./JG 1 at Parchim in February 1945. This aircraft was fitted with two 30 mm MK 108 cannon, as opposed to the later A-2 version which was equipped with MG 151/20mm cannon.

ABOVE: The first He 162 to leave Heinkel's Marienehe factory on 25 March 1945.

ABOVE RIGHT: Factory-fresh He 162 (W.Nr.120222). According to Hans Berger, then Staffelkapitän of 3./JG 1, the red arrow was only decorative and did not hold any tactical significance.

On 8 April, Parchim was bombed by the RAF. Pilots and He 162s transferred to Ludwigslust, 17 km (11 mls) south-west of Parchim. From there, several more test flights were made.

JG 1's pilots were not the only ones to experience difficulties with the He 162; ferry pilots also found problems, sometimes resulting in tragedy. At the end of March 1945, *Oblt.* Wolfgang Wollenweber who led a ferry *Kommando* received orders to deliver 15 He 162s to JG 1. His 15 pilots took over the aircraft at the Bernburg factory near Halle with a stopover at Unterschlauersbach. On 1 April three pilots – *Lt.* Büttner piloting He 162 W.Nr. 310006, *Fw.* Strauss in He 162 W.Nr. 310002 and *Uffz.* Dobrath in He 162 W.Nr. 310018 – took off from Bernburg. The next day, Dobrath returned but found it impossible to land at Unterschlauersbach, the airfield having fallen to the Americans. He was forced to make an emergency landing east of Nürnberg. On 6 April, *Lt.* Finner, *Fw.* Seeling, *Fw.* Häusel and *Uffz.* Dobrath took off for Lechfeld. They never reached their goal and their fate remains unknown.

On 11 April, *Oblt.* Wollenweber, *Ofhr.* Stenschke, *Ofhr.* Köttgen, *Uffz.* Hartung, and *Uffz.* Riemer delivered their He 162s to Ludwigslust. But during this flight *Fhr.* Mann disappeared in the Magdeburg area.

Nevertheless, the number of He 162s on JG 1's strength continued to grow. While some pilots continued making ferry flights, others carried out assessment and familiarisation flights in small formations. Progressively, they began to understand their new aircraft and learned to appreciate it despite a few early teething problems.

Lt. Hans Berger of 3./JG 1 recalls: "We considered this little aircraft with its wooden wings and large turbine on its back behind the cockpit with a degree of scepticism. Accustomed to the protection of the Fw 190's massive engine, we felt exposed and unprotected behind the thin leaf of the cockpit Plexiglas. Even more importantly, there were several weaknesses which caused us concern such as the fragile join between the wings and the fuselage. In flight, you had to pilot it with an incredible sensitivity, because the aircraft reacted to every smallest touch on the stick; she was that soft. It was especially at low speeds that the aircraft became most dangerous for it skidded easily. In just a few days, three pilots, including *Fw.* Friedrich Enderle, were killed just after take-off. *Fw.* Rolf Ackermann lost his life while landing. Once again, and even more so than in the past, the lack of training amongst the new pilots was evident. With a machine so sensitive, intuitive flying was vital.

"In order to start the engine, it was necessary to use an electric starter coupled to the turbine, by pressing on a red button. There was a loud noise often accompanied by a jet of small, spitting flames. But if the noise was loud outside the aircraft, one was aware of it only slightly in the cockpit, and even less so after take-off. You couldn't hear the slipstream, just as with a glider. The most impressive thing without doubt was the speed; 750... 800... 850... 900...km/h. I remember several exciting flights where I reached nearly 1,000 km/h at low altitude over the sandy beaches above the island of Amrum. The short range was the only handicap; 35 to 40 minutes flying duration at high altitude and by drastic economy, you could stretch it to 50 minutes. If you encountered the enemy, the order was to attack from a more elevated position. We regretted the lack of opportunities of measuring our new aircraft against enemy fighters."

Uffz. Alvo von Alvensleben, of 1./JG 1 also flew the *Volksjäger*: "When the engine was started up, an unusually loud noise came from the turbine. The aircraft, small and light, with a huge engine on its back, made such a din rolling on the runway that one was relieved when the aircraft lifted off. The wheels left the ground at a speed of 220 km/h. Acceleration was good and a normal runway sufficed. In flight, the aircraft was stable and quiet. It responded easily to the controls. In general, training speeds were between 500 and 700 km/h. In the dive, according to factory information, we could reach the speed of sound.

As for myself, I was able to reach 1,000 km/h once. We did not have the opportunity to try aerobatics with it though. Lacking experience on the type, and having doubts as to the solidity of the undercarriage, I always touched down as gently as possible. After a very short flight, it would land, and once again the noise became appalling. I flew the aircraft on ten occasions."

On 15 and 16 April, I. *Gruppe* had to quit its new base since the front line had nearly reached it. The *Gruppe* transferred to the airfield of Leck, in Schleswig-Holstein, some arriving via Husum.

Lt. Gerhard Stiemer of 3./JG 1 remembered: "On 15 April, I prepared to take-off in order to go to Leck. In readiness for a long journey, my He 162 was equipped with a 1,300 litre tank. The runway proved too short for my aircraft, burdened as it was by the additional fuel. At the very moment when my wheels finally got off the ground, the left wing collided with a radio mast. All my strength was necessary to keep control of the now very damaged aircraft. I did a U-turn and landed. On 16 April, I took off again for Leck, this time with *Uffz.* Rieder. Heavy *flak* welcomed us over Hamburg. In traversing the *flak* belt, we consumed too much fuel and had to land on the concrete runway at Husum. The following day, we left for Leck and I reached it without difficulty, but alone. Indeed, my friend Rieder crashed following a problem with the flaps. He was hospitalised. On 19 April, I took-off ahead of *Fw.* Günther Kirchner to intercept some P-47s. We had hardly reached an altitude of 50 metres, when we were attacked from the rear. Though Kirchner succeeded in ejecting his seat, the lack of altitude was not sufficient to allow his parachute to open and my comrade fell to his death. I was much luckier and managed to escape, but then I could not lower my undercarriage! I approached the airfield flying at the lowest altitude and landed as quickly as I could. 20 April: I took off with *Lt.* Berger when we saw P-47s. Upon landing, lack of fuel forced me to come down on the runway at a bad angle.

I crashed my 162 and the shock made me lose consciousness. *Oblt.* Demuth was the first to arrive at the scene of the crash and smashed in the canopy with an axe. A puff of oxygen brought me back to consciousness. Suffering injuries to my legs, I was taken away to the hospital in Leck where I joined my friend Rieder. It was in that bed that I would hear about the surrender."

On 4 May, shortly before noon, *Lt.* Rudolf Schmitt from 1. *Staffel* claimed a victory with the He 162. Again however, without any official documentation, it is impossible to confirm it.

Oblt. Demuth remembers the event: "I had heard by telephone of the crash of a British aircraft in our sector so we went by car to look for the pilot and invited him to dinner in our mess. As some of us spoke some English, we discussed aeronautical matters and our lost war, and about the qualities and shortcomings of our respective aircraft. The following morning, we were sad to see him taken away to a POW camp."

Two subsequent elements serve to place doubt on Schmitt's claim; firstly, it seems the British pilot pretended to have been the victim of a He 162, and secondly, a *flak* unit was credited with the claim.

On 8 April, II. *Gruppe* left its Fw 190s at Garz and moved to Rostock/Marienehe en route to receive training on the He 162.

Uffz. Konrad Augner of 8./JG 1: "The officers were lodged in a hotel at Warnemünde, and the other pilots on the airfield. Each morning, as workers headed for work, a bus or wagon collected us and took us to Marienehe airfield. It was an unusual place with three runways set out in a triangle in the middle of marsh land. First of all, we

Oblt. Emil Demuth, Staffelkapitän of 3./JG 1, poses in front of the fin and rudder of his He 162 A-2, W.Nr. 120074, which carries 16 kill markings gained on Fw 190s.

From left to right: Uffz. Brune, Fw. Ackermann, Klein, Fw. Kirchner and Fw. Köhne all members of 3./JG 1 in mid-April 1945. Ackermann and Kirchner, the two most experienced pilots, were killed on 23 and 19 April 1945 respectively, at the controls of He 162s.

ABOVE: *A He 162 of I./JG 1 with a black-white-red nose at Ludwigslust, April 1945.*

BELOW: *Following the Allied bombing of Parchim, I./JG 1 moved to Ludwigslust in mid-April 1945. Note here that the camouflage of He 162 A-2 'White 21' of 1./JG 1 differs to the other two aircraft in the picture; the demarcation of the upper surface camouflage pattern stops level with the cockpit. Note also the tricoloured nose as well as the arrows and the red tip at the front of the engine housing.*

received theoretical training on the aircraft we would be flying. Then we learned to start the engine, increase the throttle progressively, and move onto the runway. We sat in this aircraft as if in a glider. Starting the engine was a completely different procedure to that of the Bf 109. The revs had to be increased slowly, while holding the aircraft still with the help of the brakes, up to the moment when one decided that there was sufficient power for take-off. Releasing the brakes, take-off was achieved at around 180 km/h. After retracting the undercarriage, we also retracted the flaps. We climbed at around 450-500 km/h. This aircraft had a mortal fault; at less than 300 km/h you had to be on your guard against tight turns. In this case, the aileron constrained the circulation of air around the turbine, the He 162 skidded and fell like a leaf without any possibility of correcting it. Generally, we only flew for about 35 minutes at fairly low level. However we also made several flights at 8,000 metres. We would then be in the air for over an hour. The manoeuvrability of the aircraft was good. For landing, we approached the runway at about 250-260 km/h, and touched down at 200. It was a totally new flying sensation.

"On 24 April, I was on the airfield looking skywards when a catastrophe occurred. Our *Gruppenkommandeur*, *Hptm*. Dähne, did not seem to have confidence in this machine, and I think he neglected his training. That day, at about 16.00, he took off. We followed his manoeuvres – he was not flying higher than 500 metres. He started to turn, and the aircraft began to skid. I then saw the aircraft somersault. Small pieces of glass shone in the sun, and a trail of white smoke came from the turbine. The He 162 began to lose height. It fell like a dead leaf and crashed in the marsh at the mouth of the Warne. Our *Gruppenkommandeur* had probably tried to bale out without first having jettisoned the canopy, and had smashed his skull. That would explain the splinters of glass. We immediately jumped into boats to come to his aid. We searched in vain …"

Major Werner Zober, a veteran of the Spanish Civil War and holder of the Spanish Cross with Diamonds, was appointed *Hptm*. Dähne's successor.

The Peoples' Fighter 295

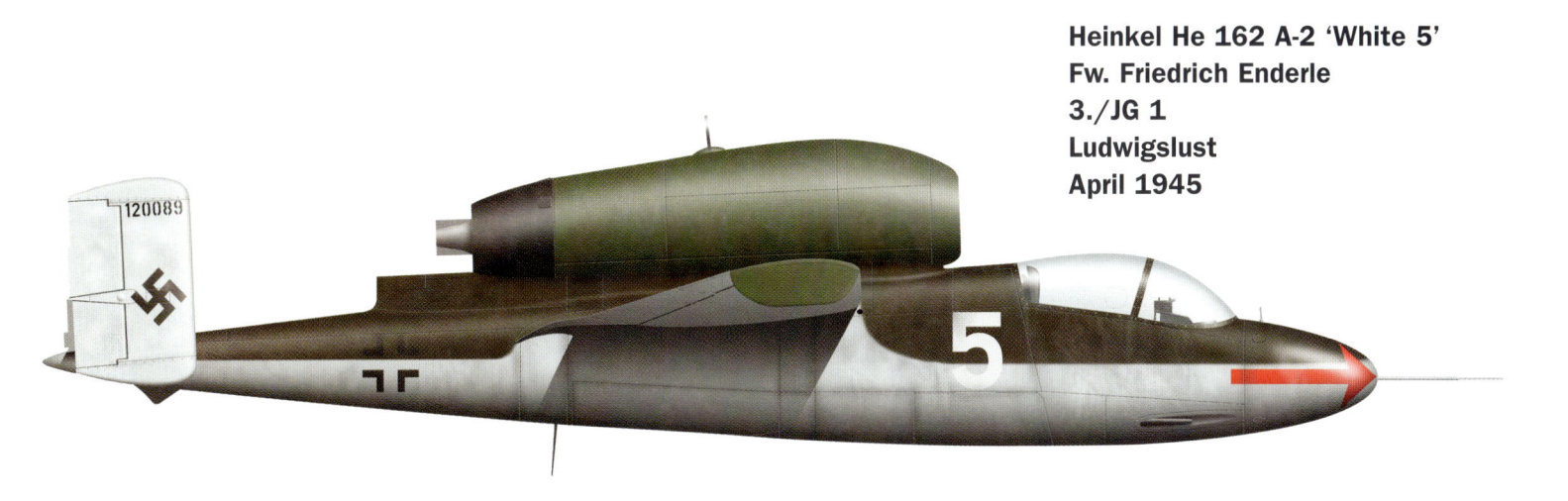

Heinkel He 162 A-2 'White 5'
Fw. Friedrich Enderle
3./JG 1
Ludwigslust
April 1945

LEFT AND BELOW: Ludwigslust, 13 April 1945. Fw. Friedrich Enderle of 3./JG 1 and the aircraft in which he would experience calamity. He crashed shortly after take-off.

Chapter Twenty-Four

The End

April – May 1945

"Since January 1945, the war could be summed up for us as a succession of road and rail journeys. At the beginning of April we were at Ludwigslust. We then received the order to move to Husum. Having waited for nightfall, we set off. We were four officers in one car; *Oberleutnant* Wilhelm Krebs (Technical Officer of I. *Gruppe*); *Major* Bernd Gallowitsch (an Austrian *Ritterkreuzträger* with 64 victories from JG 51 and recently posted to the unit by the *General der Jagdflieger*); *Hauptmann* Hans Bleser (HQ Company Chief) and myself *Hauptmann* Ludwig Siegfried, supply officer of I. *Gruppe*. We travelled for an hour before we were hit head-on by another car. This happened frequently due to the poor headlights in the darkness. Krebs and Gallowitsch were slightly injured and, more through good luck than judgement, we made it to Husum. It was crowded with retreating troops in northern Germany. We could spend only the rest of the night there. The following day, at midday, we finally reached Leck, where the remainder of the *Gruppe* were established."

Viennese Major and Ritterkreuzträger Bernd Gallowitsch seen here at Leck in May 1945, became Staffelkapitän of 7./JG 1 on 1 February 1945. At the end of the war, he was Staffelkapitän of 4./JG 1. He was awarded the Ritterkreuz whilst with JG 51.

On the afternoon of 1 May, *Stab* and II./JG 1 hurriedly left Marienehe since the Russians had reached the Heinkel installations. The pilots joined I. *Gruppe* at Leck after a stop-over at Kaltenkirchen.

Oblt. Wolfgang Wollenweber of 3./JG 1 recalled: "I remember perfectly the last ferry flight of He 162s taking off from Marienehe. I assumed command. We had to get the aircraft out by ourselves from the jigs and bring them to the runway. I had to organise everything personally, eventually finding a tractor for the task. As we lacked two He 162s, I had prepared a Fieseler Storch in which I planned to escape the Russians. I put my leather coat and some provisions into the cockpit. After having accompanied *Uffz.* Riehl to the take-off point, I rejoined an NCO. We were quickly joined again by Riehl who had had to land back with his deficient Heinkel. Fortunately, despite the fact he had landed in a bomb crater, he was unhurt. In the mean time, someone had stolen my leather coat and the provisions. Before Riehl's take off, I had offered the third seat in the Fieseler to the engineer, Gundermann. But with Riehl back (we were now four), an attempt to take-off in the small machine designed only for two or three occupants was almost collective suicide. We gave it a shot, despite everything, and we rushed down the runway – well quite slowly really – in order to take-off. At the moment the wheels began to lift off, a *Nachkommando* (rear unit) exploded the fuel tanks near the runway. The blast pushed us into the air! We landed at Leck on 1 May at 13.30, not without having been mistaken as a target by the *flak* for our shipping in Lübeck Bay."

The last re-organisation of JG 1 took place at this time. I. and II. *Gruppen* were redesignated I. (*Einsatz*)/JG 1 and II. (*Sammel*)/JG 1. The command structure was as follows:

Geschwaderstab *Oberst* Herbert Ihlefeld

Stab, I. Gruppe	*Major* Werner Zober
1. Staffel	*Hauptmann* Heinz Künneke
2. Staffel	*Hauptmann* Wolfgang Ludewig
3. Staffel	*Oberleutnant* Emil Demuth.
Stab, II. Gruppe	*Hauptmann* Rahe
4. Staffel	*Major* Bernd Gallowitsch
5. Staffel	*Hauptmann* Bergholz
6. Staffel	*Oberleutnant* Zipprecht

These two *Gruppen* recorded a total of 50 pilots on strength and an equivalent number of aircraft.

Uffz. Konrad Augner of 2./JG 1: "Our commanding officer, Ihlefeld, advised us of Hitler's death and told us to stay together until the Allies captured our airfield. By so doing, no harm could come to us. He also told us that he no longer had the right to retain us. Everyone was free to go. I don't believe a single person left."

Hptm. Ludwig Siegfried of *Stab*, I. *Gruppe*: "On 5 May, at around 08.00 hours we received the order from HQ *Luftwaffe Mitte* to cease action. We each placed one or two kilos of explosives in our aircraft. In the evening we received a new order; we were to leave our aircraft intact and to deliver them to the enemy. During the night we removed the explosives. On 6 May, the British reached the aerodrome, which we had by then evacuated. We were on the way to Flensburg, to a camp at Schmörholm. Arms were collected and only the officers retained their pistols. On 8 May, the Allies took over the airfield and shared out our He 162s. They also took the technical personnel, who were required to keep the aircraft in flying condition. On 25 May, our 25 female auxiliaries were released. Myself, I was set free on 13 July. Five days later, at 22.00 hours, I reached my family home at Wesermünde."

Oblt. Wolfgang Wollenweber of 3./JG 1: "When the Allied pilots came to Leck to take over our He 162s, *Oberst* Ihlefeld ordered me to explain to them the way to pilot these aircraft. To do this, I ordered the technicians to put my 'White 3' into flight readiness. Nevertheless, my 'show flight' was cancelled, the British test pilot considering that my help would not be necessary. Indeed, he made a perfect flight. After its landing, he said to us how much he was enthusiastic about the aircraft. My He 162 was refuelled for me but I would never receive authorisation to fly it. Surely, they were still suspicious of a German pilot?"

For III. *Gruppe*, the end of the war was more eventful. In mid-April, when it was envisaged that the unit's pilots would start their conversion training on the He 162, they relinquished their aircraft and took up residence at Markgrafenheide-Warnemünde, near Rostock. Ground personnel took on charge several He 162s there, but they did not have time to prepare them for pilot training. From 24 April, III. *Gruppe* was officially disbanded. The most experienced pilots were transferred to other units, for example *Ofw.* Fritz Haspel and *Uffz.* Hugo Hausotter were posted to 5./JG 27, whom they joined in the Flensburg area. Some of the ground personnel were sent to Neustrelitz where they had to change their *Luftwaffe* uniforms for that of the infantry. They received weapons and were told to make their way to Berlin to take part in its defence. A counter-order quickly arrived. Berlin was encircled, so they had to defend Neustrelitz.

Fw. Ernst Wedel, was a III. *Gruppe* technician: "We were posted to the west of the city where white smoke was rising up into the sky. Artillery and Russian armour were moving forwards. Our retreat west was made possible by the intervention of our tanks and members of the Hitler Youth armed with *Panzerfaust*. We didn't wait for the order to retreat. During the night of 7-8 May, our battalion, named '*Eisen*' was dissolved. We were given our papers and were told that the Russians were 100 metres to the east with the Americans a similar distance to the west. Naturally we turned west and were very quickly captured, in the Neustadt-Kleve area."

At the end of April, the disbanded III./JG 1 still had about 40 pilots and 70 ground personnel on strength.

Uffz. Dietmar Hillmer of 11./JG 1: "On the last day of April 1945, the commander of the airfield at Markgrafenheide told us that we would be engaged in the defence of the airfield. On the morning of 1 May, our III. *Gruppe* was alone, the units which should have been alongside us having left during the night for Denmark. We were without arms or munitions, apart from several revolvers. Our commander, *Hauptmann* Moldenhauer, took the decision to evacuate his men to the west. After a good breakfast, we shouldered our packs and started marching. Our objective was Leck. The first resting place was going to be Doberan. Our column was rapidly mixed up with a large mass of refugees. We reached Warnow-Fähre and headed towards Warnemünde. The group began to split up. I was walking in front. The commander told me and a comrade to try to regroup the men. The first to arrive dropped their baggage at the foot of a concrete wall two metres high and headed for a naval refreshment centre for their evening rations. My friend and I had hardly put down our packs when, suddenly, the war caught up with us. The sounds of battle came from the west. That was the way we were heading! All around us, people were running. My friend and I calmly remained seated whilst enemy fighters carried out strafing attacks close by. We searched the horizon – the sky remained empty. New bursts of fire were heard. Jumping up, we climbed onto the wall

FAR LEFT: Following the end of hostilities, these four officers of JG 1 await their final release by the Allies. From left to right: Lt. Hans Berger, Oblt. Emil Demuth, Lt. Gerhard Hanf and Oblt. Wilhelm Krebs. On the tent peg, the three well known emblems of JG 1.

Following the dissolution of III./JG 1 at the end of April 1945, several experienced pilots of III./JG 1 were posted to other units. Fw. Hugo Hausotter and Ofw. Fritz Haspel, who arrived at 10./JG 1 three years earlier, were transferred to 5./JG 27.

behind which were the tracks of Warnemünde station. Behind it, Russian tanks were firing. We dropped down and, without having recovered from our surprise, saw our commander with six men. They were looking for their packs. *'What are you doing here?,* asked Moldenhauer, *'Come with us, quickly.'* We picked up our packs and rejoined the small group. We headed for the landing stage and the jetty. From there, five naval boats were leaving, full of refugees and soldiers. The first four were heading out of the port, the fifth had just cut loose from the quay. The skipper saw us and told us to jump. One and a half metres from the quay there were wooden moorings. It was a metre higher than the quay, and it was not a simple matter to reach the boat. The boat continued to head away. We had to jump from mooring to mooring to reach it. Four strong hands lifted us on board. Hardly had the last of us got on board than a violent shaking took us by surprise. The boat put on full steam to escape the port. Our ability to reach the boat was not due to any athletic prowess on our part, but to a real fear which gave us 'wings'!

"On the beach, at the foot of the Warnemünde lighthouse, the first Russian tanks rolled past. They had seen us. The marines took up their action stations and returned fire. We 'passengers' took cover. To the right, and from behind, two aircraft appeared at great speed. The gunners quickly opened fire on them. We recognised them as Arado 234s and we shouted: *'They're ours!'* The firing stopped immediately. The four other boats did likewise. Meanwhile, we had succeeded in getting out of the range of the Russians. They fired a last salvo, which posed no danger to us. One craft which had been hit in the stern was towed by one of our other friends. Out at sea, soldiers and refugees transferred onto a Danish cargo vessel. Anything that was not necessary was abandoned. I only possessed what I was carrying. The ships separated. Ours followed the coastline to the west at a safe distance from the shore. In the early evening, anxiety returned; we were passing through a minefield and saw the anti-submarine nets in the port of Wismar. The mines were pushed away behind us by using poles. Strange sights for a flyer! We docked at Wismar, 50 kilometres west of Rostock, without knowing how much further the Russians had advanced. The enemy was no longer with us. The captain was able to bring his family on board. We sailed again and began our games with the mines once more. On the morning of 2 May, we followed the coast and entered the port of Orth, where the ship was camouflaged with fishing nets. The flotilla was replenished with fuel and food. We spent two quiet days on the Baltic, the 'peace' only broken by enemy fighter-bombers heading for inland targets. Several times we thought we had been spotted. However thanks to the ice-cool nerves of our captain, we remained safe from attack. In the evening we entertained our saviour.

"Twenty-four hours later, our captain announced that he would land us at Kappeln. Under cover of darkness, the camouflage nets were removed and we put out to sea. During the night the flotilla cruised at slow speed through the Kiel straits. In the distance we saw flashes. The poor city was undergoing further bombardment. At dawn on 4 May, the other ships had disappeared. Our vessel entered the mouth of the Schlei and zig-zagged to avoid the mines and anti-submarine nets. We landed at Kappeln and left the marines. The sun was shining, and we saluted the vessel, which was moving off. In front of a hangar, there was a long queue. As it seemed to be involved in distribution of some kind, we approached with interest. It was a naval depot whose contents were being distributed to the population. While our commander spoke to the Quartermaster, we spoke to some young girls. I learned that my father, *Major* Hillmer, had his quarters nearby. I caught him by surprise while he was shaving. The reunion was very moving; he finally had one of his three sons returned to him. I introduced him to my friends. He put a vehicle at our disposal. Our small group then split up. I remained with my friend while the others, including Moldenhauer, set off in the direction of Leck to rejoin the unit's other two *Gruppen*. My career as a flyer finished in that manner – somewhat abruptly, but with a certain amount of luck. Interned, I was released by the British at Hamburg, at the end of August 1945."

Thus the story of *Jagdgeschwader* 1 ended amidst the general chaos of a destroyed Germany. A new fight would start soon for the survivors of JG 1; the daily and difficult search for a piece of bread. Only the luckiest would be able to continue the studies which the outbreak of war had interrupted, for most of them would have to relearn the realities of a life of peace and rebuild a ruined land.

Numerous Luftwaffe units surrendered at Leck and the Allies discovered an enormous number of German aircraft and among them, the jet fighters in which their captors showed great interest. This He 162 was taken on charge by the French.

LEFT: He 162 'Red 1' (W.Nr.120077) at Leck, late April 1945. This was the aircraft of Lt. Gerhard Hanf, Staffelkapitän of 2./JG 1, the unit with whom he made his 17th and last flight in a Volksjäger on 29 April. Note the wolf's head emblem of III./JG 77. It was with this unit that he undertook his first combat mission before his Staffel was transferred to I./JG 1 in Summer 1944.

BELOW: This rear view of a He 162 photographed after the German surrender offers the observer a characteristic silhouette of the Volksjäger.

LEFT: He 162 A-2 'Yellow 1' (W.Nr.120223) of 3./JG 1 at Ludwigslust at the end of April 1945. Note the canopy ventilation panel visible on the open hood and the red arrow on the nose.

300 JG 1 – Defenders of the Reich

LEFT: Hptm. Heinz Künneke poses in front of a He 162 'White 5' of 1./JG 1. The unit had just adopted an emblem which was reminiscent of the one carried by Bf 109s in the early months of the war.

ABOVE AND LEFT: He 162 A-2s of 1./JG 1 lined up at Leck shortly before the end of the war.

Heinkel He 162 A-2 'White 1'
1./JG 1
Leck
May 1945

A line-up of Volksjäger of I./JG 1 at Leck, May 1945. In the foreground is He 162 A-2 'Yellow 4' (W.Nr.120067) of 3./JG 1.

LEFT: *Officers in front of their He 162s at Leck, May 1945. From left to right: Major Zober, Oberst Ihlefeld, Hptm. Künneke, Oblt. Demuth, Major Gallowitsch, Oblt. Wind, Hptm. Strasen (hidden and Kommandeur of III./JG 4) and Hptm. Ludewig (in leather coat).*

RIGHT: *With He 162s lined up behind them (from left to right) Hptm. Wolfgang Ludewig (Staffelkapitän of 2./JG 1), Major Werner Zober (Gruppenkommandeur of I./JG 1), Hptm. Heinz Künneke (Staffelkapitän of 1./JG 1) and Oblt. Emil Demuth (Staffelkapitän of 3./JG 1) pose for one their last photographs of the war.*

ABOVE: The lion holding a yellow '3' emblem was introduced by 3./JG 1 during the last weeks of the war by Lt. Gerhard Stiemer in honour of his home city, Danzig.

ABOVE: He 162 'Yellow 5' of 3./JG 1 probably photographed after the war. Note the three emblems under the cockpit representing the epic story of I./JG 1: the pink demon emerging from clouds adopted in 1942 by IV./JG 1 (subsequently I./JG 1), the Lion of Danzig appearing on the flank of He 162s of 3./JG 1 and the winged '1' of JG 1 carried on the unit's aircraft from the end of 1943.

LEFT AND ABOVE: He 162 A-2 'White 3' is restored to flight-worthiness at Leck on 15 or 16 May 1945 under the attentive eye of Oblt. Wolfgang Wollenweber. In effect, Wollenweber would teach British test pilots how to handle the He 162. Note the 20 mm. cannon, the red ring at the front of the engine housing and the absence of the red arrow on the nose.

Index

Ackermann, Fw., Rolf 292
Adolph, Oblt., Walter 9, 10, 19, 20, 22
Alvensleben, Uffz., Alvo von 283, 292
Andersens, P/O, Alex 102
Auer, Uffz., Alfred 74
Augner, Uffz., Konrad 285, 293, 296
Bach, Ofw., Otto 103, 104, 105, 127, 140, 147, 151, 158, 160, 166, 181, 198, 227-79, 260, 264, 265
Bahl, Fw., Fritz 31, 32, 36, 182
Balthasar, Oblt., Wilhelm 9, 10, 12, 14, 15, 18, 19, 20, 22
Bär, Obstlt., Heinz 207, 211, 212, 216, 217, 225, 227, 228, 229, 230, 233, 235, 236, 246, 291
Barann, Ofw., Leo-Lothar 261, 286
Becker, Oblt., Karl 105, 127, 128, 158, 160
Behrens, Uffz., Gerhard 282
Beise, Hptm., Günter 55
Berger, Lt., Hans 149, 181, 196, 206, 209-11, 227, 269, 282, 292, 293
Bergholz, Hptm., 296
Beyer, Fw., Rudolf 52
Biederbick, Helmut 213, 228
Bier, Hptm. 53
Biermann, Uffz., Herbert 96
Bilfinger, Oblt., Fritz 254, 255, 264, 265
Bindseil, Fw., 236
Blesser, Hptm., Hans 296
Bock, Oblt., Eberhard 40, 45, 46, 53
Boettcher, Ogfr. 74, 170
Born, Uffz., Heinz 86
Bools, W/O 56
Borchers, Oblt. 40
Brakebush, Uffz., Herbert 54, 55, 67
Brandt, Uffz, Hans 20
Braun, Uffz. 32
Braune Oblt., Ehrard 15
Braxator, Fw., Horst 15, 20
Bristow, F/O 56
Bruhnke, Uffz., Ehrard 103
Brumund, Uffz., Kurt 160
Brunner, Fw., Wolfgang 193
Brünnler, Johann 247
Brustellin, Hptm., Hans-Heinrich 48
Bucek, Uffz. 79, 81, 84
Buchholz, Lt., Erich 58, 64, 69, 77, 88, 118, 194, 196, 233, 234
Buchholz, Lt., Günther 233
Buchholz, Oblt., Max 40, 44, 54, 55, 58, 64, 69, 77, 88, 89, 141
Bugaj, Fw., Karl 56, 82, 102, 130
Bülow-Bothkamp von, Major, Harry 6
Burath, Lt., Eberhard 56, 104, 126, 131, 136, 139, 158, 159, 160, 206, 209, 211, 212, 216, 227, 229
Burckhardt, Lutz-Wilhelm 207, 229, 230, 254
Büttner, Lt., 292
Cantillion, P/O, André 86
Capito, Maj., Günther 282, 283
Chojnacki, F/O 281
Churchill, Prime Minister, Winston 102, 225
Clade, Uffz., Emil 19
Dahl, Obstlt., Walter 291
Dähne, Hptm., Paul-Heinrich 285, 294
Decker, Gefr. 166
Dedow, Lt., 194
Deklerk, Uffz., Bernhard 25, 32
Delannay, 1. Sgt, Roger 18
Demetz, Uffz., Leo 105

Demuth, Oblt., Emil 181, 187, 193, 194, 210, 212, 213, 216, 226, 230, 259, 261, 264-68, 282-84, 293, 296
Deterra, Lt. 54, 85
Diesem, Oblt., Rudolf 266
Diesselhorst, Oblt., Walter 44, 53, 64
Dietrich, Oberwerksmeister 64
Dilling, Ofw., Gustav 250
Dobislav, Oblt., Max 10, 15
Dobrath, Uffz., Walter 250-52, 292
Dobrick, Fw., Erich 15, 37
Dolenga, Hptm., Werner 37, 46, 52
Doppler, Uffz., Alwin 105, 118
Döring, Obgfr., 263
Dosch, Uffz., Hubert 211
Doyle, Col., James L 235
Dürr, Lt., Alfred 286
Düsterbeck, Lt., Johannes 182
Dutel, Lt., Erwin 18
Eberhard, Ofw., Peter 125, 140
Eberle, Oblt., Friedrich 46, 49, 51, 53, 62, 65, 83, 185, 187, 196, 207, 210, 228, 230
Eder ,Georg 207, 227, 229, 230, 233, 235, 236, 246, 252
Eh, Lt., Herbert 160, 183
Ehlers, Oblt., Hans 55, 56, 126, 148, 149, 151, 185, 186, 194, 196, 198, 199, 200, 209, 210, 213, 216, 229, 230, 246, 251, 264-69, 280
Eichel-Streiber von, Oblt., Diethelm 41
Eichner, Lt., Eberhard 52
Einberger, Uffz., Rudolf 164, 187
Eisenach, Oblt., Franz 53
Ell, Gefr., Konrad 130
Emmerich, Uffz., Felix 104, 105, 126, 128, 187
Enderle, Fw., Friedrich 265, 292
Endrizzi, Lt., Karl 55
Engleder, Lt., Rudolf 149, 150, 158, 160, 163, 170, 181, 185, 186, 187, 188, 193, 194, 198, 229
Eriksen, FLt., Marius 125
Ernst, Oblt. Wolfgang 238, 252, 254
Ertmann, Lt., Horst 158, 267
Faber, Hptm., Alfred 194
Faber, Fw., Klaus 10, 15
Falck, Hptm., Wolfgang 8, 36
Falkensammer, Hptm., Egon 103
Fest, Uffz., Wilhelm 116
Feustel, Lt., Hans 179, 181
Fick, Ofw. 149
Fiedler, Ogfr. 167, 170
Finger, Ofgr. Martin 229
Finner, Lt., 292
Fischer, Fw. 32
Flecks, Uffz., Reinhard 54, 55, 67, 102, 105, 113, 120, 149, 158, 181, 199, 213, 230, 255, 256, 268
Flemming, Uffz., Gerhard 74, 81, 84
Förster, Lt., Richard 268
Framm, Oblt., Rainer 53, 56, 95, 125, 194
Franzisket, Lt., Ludwig 15, 18, 20, 21
Frey, Oblt., Hugo 56, 76, 93, 103, 105, 113, 115, 116
Fricke, Gefr. 74
Friedrich, Erich (BMW) 72
Fritzsche, Uffz., Alfred 282
Fröhlich, Ofw., Georg 178, 193, 248

Fuchs, Uffz., Heinz 123, 185, 198, 207, 209, 216
Gall, Gefr., Bruno 182, 184
Galland, Gen., Adolf 20, 44, 45, 48, 117, 235
Gallowitsch, Maj. Bernd 296
Geberth, Uffz., Kurt 234
Gebser, Fw., Hans-Joachim 235
Gerhardt, Lt., Dieter 37, 43, 46, 51, 95, 105, 112, 113, 114, 115, 116
Gerhardt, Ofw., Werner 24, 41
Gillert, Fw 19
Goffin, Lt., Charles 18
Gollob, Obst., Gordon 291
Gordy, Capt., James 252
Göring, Reichsmarshall, Hermann 185, 194, 225, 246, 250
Grabmann, Oberst, Walter 54
Grasser, Maj., Hartmann 234-36, 238
Greber, Uffz., 236
Greuner, Oblt., Heinrich 283
Griener, Ofw., Albert 54
Grislawski, Hptm., Alfred 194, 196, 198, 199, 200, 209, 210, 229, 230, 247, 254, 255, 264
Grosser, Lt., Heinz 41
Grütz, Uffz., Erwin 55, 82
Guisgand, Capt. 18
Gutowski, Hptm., Werner 41, 61, 85, 86, 119
Hachtel, Lt., 291
Hackbarth, Hptm., Hans Georg 280-82
Haenel, Uffz., Herbert 103
Hahn von, Hptm., Hans 40, 54, 64
Hahn, Fw., Karl 281
Halbey, Lt., Hans 159, 267
Hamann, Uffz., Horst 90
Hamann, Fw. Josef 58
Hänert, Uffz., Lothar 212
Hanf, Lt., Gerhard 254, 264, 268
Haninger, Fw., Rudolf 87, 103, 123, 148, 186, 194
Hanke, Uffz., Heinz 59, 85, 86, 105, 109
Hardt, Oblt., Friedrich 124, 150, 154, 166, 168
Hartung, Uffz., 292
Hasenfuss, Uffz., Günther 158
Haspel, Uffz., Fritz 55, 79, 81, 158, 160, 161, 179, 212, 216, 230, 255, 297
Häusel, Fw., 292
Hausotter, Uffz., Hugo 255, 297
Heckmann, Lt., Günther 236, 238, 247, 251, 261, 264, 266
Heesen, Ofw., Ernst 56, 77, 88, 102, 126
Heidrich, Uffz., 283
Heidrich, Oblt., (Hans) Werner 55, 56
Heimbach, Ofw., Roman 231
Hempel, Fw., Heinz 183
Hempler, Uffz. 194
Henschel, Hptm., Julius 56
Hentschel, Uffz.118
Hermichen, Rolf 225, 226
Hewitt, Capt., John 252
Heydrich, SS-Gruppenführer, Reinhard 32
Hildenbrand, Uffz., Gerhard 286
Hillmer, Uffz., Dietmar 297
Hillmer, Major 298
Hitler, Adolf 9, 18, 32
Hoeckner, Hptm., Walter 126, 160, 179, 181, 185, 186, 187, 195, 196, 207

Hoës, Uffz. 54, 86, 119
Hofmann, Uffz., Fritz 250, 282
Hoge, Fw., Wilhelm 188
Hollmann, Gefr. 74, 130
Homfeld, Uffz., Hans-Hasso 233
Houwald von, Oblt., Heinrich 9
Hoyer, Uffz., Alfred 186
Hübl, Uffz., Rudolf 126, 149, 162, 163, 170, 183, 186, 192, 212, 216, 227, 233, 234, 252
Hummer, Uffz., Werner 231
Huppertz, Oblt., Herbert 41
Husser, Ofw., Fritz 149, 150, 155, 159, 168, 172
Hutter, Fw., Georg 53, 55, 58, 64, 77, 88, 105, 140, 151, 158, 183, 267
Ibel, Oberst, Max 18, 44
Ibing, Lt., Kurt 174, 254
Ickes, Uffz., Friedrich 263
Ihlefeld, Obstlt., Herbert 247, 255, 260, 281, 282, 296
Jackson, Sgt. 56
Janke, Oblt., Jochen 265, 266
Januschwski, Fw. 15
Job, Uffz., Alois 41, 54, 58, 102, 108, 118
Johannides, Lt., Ernst von 282
Johnen, Fw. 32, 33, 43
Just, Lt. Gottfried 267, 268
Kageneck von, Lt, Erbo Graf 19, 20
Kaiser, Uffz., Erich 48, 54, 149, 163, 170
Kaiser, Ofw., Herbert 207, 230, 236, 254, 261
Kamutzki, Gefr. Johannes 255
Kaniss, Ofw., Hans 255, 259
Kaschichke, Lt., Rudolf 212
Kasuhn, Hptm. Friedrich 254
Kehrle, Fw., Josef 69, 77, 143, 153, 160, 161, 164, 176, 194
Kettner, Oberartz 261
Kienitz, Hptm., Walter 24
Kijewski, Hptm., Herbert 41, 54, 85, 123, 124, 132
Kind, Albert 210
Kinsky, Ogfr., Franz 151
Kirchhoff, Uffz. 81, 84, 198
Kirchmayr von, Oblt., Rüdiger 71, 72, 123, 124, 125, 141, 145, 148, 149, 179, 185, 209, 216, 227, 228, 233, 234, 236, 238, 255, 259
Kirchner, Uffz., Günther 44, 56, 64, 74, 77, 83, 86, 158, 209, 293
Kirstein, Oblt., Karl-Heinz 15, 22
Klints, Fw., Harrijs 282
Klöpper, Oblt., Heinz (Heinrich) 124, 150, 179, 184, 187, 193, 194, 196, 197
Knespel, Uffz., Karl 84, 149, 170, 172
Knoke, Lt., Heinz 37, 38, 43, 46, 51, 56, 105, 112, 113, 115, 116, 128, 261-264
Knoll, Fhr., Gustav 231
Knöller, Fw., Wilhelm 93
Koch, Fw., Fritz 109
Koch, Uffz., Günter 229
Koch, Oblt., Harry 41, 46, 59, 113, 120, 126, 148, 149, 158, 159, 160, 179, 181, 186, 187, 194, 196, 198, 199, 207
Köditz, Hptfw., Waldemar 163
Köhne, Uffz., Walter 151, 195, 198, 199, 211, 212, 227, 230

Kolschek, Uffz. 56, 120
Koplik, Lt., Franz 229, 230, 236, 237, 248, 260
Körner, Uffz., Gefr. Josef 238
Kortzfleisch von, Ofhr., Bernhard 186
Kotiza, Oblt., Eugen 149, 179, 185, 193, 194
Költgen, Ofhr., 292
Krakowitzer, Lt., Friedrich 252
Krause, Uffz. 24
Krauter, Uffz. 261
Krebs, Oblt., Wilhelm 127, 296
Kretschmer, Wolfgang 226, 227
Kromer, Fw. 111
Küchler, Uffz. 105, 128
Kuhn, Gefr. 32
Künneke, Hptm., Heinz 296
Kunze, Uffz., Bernhard 149, 156, 157, 170, 171, 182, 184, 185, 193, 194, 198, 199, 209
Küpper, Fw., Heinz 44, 51, 64
Lacha, Lt., Martin 63, 75, 93, 125, 126, 158, 160, 181, 186, 194, 198
Lammich, Oblt., Heinz 254
Lass, Lt., Hans 21, 23
Laun, Fw., Hans 79, 81, 149, 160
Leesmann, Hptm., Karl-Heinz 124, 132, 142, 146, 150, 154, 155, 158, 159, 168, 181, 182
Lehmann, Uffz., Hans 104, 120, 150
Lent, Major, Helmut 146, 168
Leonhardt, Oblt., Walter 55, 102, 104
Lindenschmid, Fw., Albert 187, 207
Liper, Ofw., 209
Loch, Fw. 252
Löfgen, Ofw., Richard 166
Löhr, Uffz. 103, 128, 160
London, Cptn., C. 160
Losigkeit, Oblt., Fritz 46, 49, 53, 55, 81, 123, 125, 132, 138, 140
Lück, Lt., Heinz-Günther 149, 160, 163, 168, 186
Luckenbach, Hptm., Siegfried 124, 150, 158, 159, 166, 168
Ludewig, Hptm., Wolfgang 285, 296
Luepke, Lt.Hans-Joachim 264, 268
Lüth, Ofw., Detlev 41, 53, 55, 90, 104, 123, 158, 160, 193, 194, 196, 199
Lützow, Oberst, Günther 123, 132
Maier, Hptm., Horst 250
Mann, Fhr., 292
Mann, Lt., Erwin 12, 19, 21
Manstein von, General, Erich 18
Marshall, F/L 56
Martens, St.Fw., Rudolf 210
Martin, Ogfr. 170
Marxen, Lt., Peter 105, 160, 172
Maul, Ofw., Werner 31, 32, 34, 36, 37, 39, 43, 96
Maximow, Uffz., Hans 252
Mayer, Obstlt., Egon 234
Mayer, Uffz., Rudolf 104, 105, 106, 128
Meckel, Oblt., Helmut 40
Meinhoff, Oblt., Hans-Gottfried 281, 283
Meissmer, Uffz., Hans 54, 67, 105, 125, 154, 175, 181, 183
Meyer, Oblt., Wolfgang 255
Michalke, Uffz. 118
Michalski, Uffz., August 170, 280
Mickel, Fw., Rudolf 24, 55
Mietho, Uffz., Erwin 199, 209
Miksch, Uffz., Alfred 158, 159, 164, 165, 176, 196, 198
Milliken, Lt., Robert C. 253
Mix, Major, Erich 25, 29, 30, 32, 39, 55, 123
Mohler, Uffz., Rene 31
Mohr, Oblt., Hans 123, 124, 133, 145
Moldenhauer, Hptm. Harald 265, 266, 297, 298

Mölders, Oberst, Werner 44
Moritz, Oblt., Wilhelm 44, 45, 53, 62, 76, 82, 95
Moser, Uffz., Werner 254, 255
Müller, Oblt. Helmut 265
Muller, Oblt., Kurt 24
Munger, Lt., Paul 253
Munz, Lt., Hans 56, 127
Negressus, Uffz. 210
Nelleskamp, Fw. 53
Nette, Fw., Bodo 114, 128
Neuendorf, Fw. 118
Neumann, Lt., Herbert 231, 265, 285
Neuner, Lt., Herbert 264, 266
Nickisch, Uffz., Ferdinand von 250
Niedereichholz, Fw., Kurt 48, 67, 72, 126, 148, 193
Nietzsche, Fw., Walter 191
Nöcker, Uffz., Heinrich 24, 27, 28, 57
Nowotny, Maj., Walter 206
Oesau, Obstlt., Walter 194, 199, 207, 209-12, 216, 217, 225-27, 230, 234-36
Olejnik, Oblt., Robert 40, 43, 48, 53, 54, 55, 70, 88, 126, 148, 149, 158, 163, 179, 180, 181, 185, 187
Oswald, Uffz., Wolf 212, 261, 265, 269
Overhagen, Oblt., Heinrich 181, 194, 196, 209
Pancritius, Lt., Hans 60, 118
Pauly, Ofw. 32
Peine, Uffz., Wilhelm 234
Peltz, Gen.Maj., Dietrich 280
Penke, Gefr., 236, 248
Pfeiffer, Fw., Willi 126
Philipp, Major, Hans 123, 125, 126, 132, 134, 146, 159, 179, 186, 187
Piffer, Fw., Anton-Rudolf 56, 85, 149, 160, 185, 186, 187, 193, 196, 198, 199, 210, 228, 233, 234, 236, 250, 251
Pirkenseer, Ogfr., Franz 109
Pissarski, Uffz., Georg 148
Platzer, Uffz., Ludwig 55, 84, 93
Pleines, Uffz., Walter 217, 237
Plummer, Lt., Horace 252
Pomperger, Uffz., Johann 228
Pörsch, Oblt., 268
Praetz, Lt., Dieter 150
Quack, Lt., Meinhard 229
Rademacher, Fw. 57
Rahe. Hptm, 296
Rahner Uffz., Erich 255
Rathenow, Uffz., Johannes 55, 76, 79, 80, 81, 84, 127, 149, 163, 170, 186, 187, 193, 194, 196
Rathofer, Uffz., Fritz 250
Rau, Uffz. 170
Rauhaus, Uffz., Rudolf 56, 56, 116, 125, 149, 185, 187, 210, 216
Reichardt, Major, Hellmuth 6
Reichstein, Uffz., Egon 84, 102, 118
Reinecke, Hptm., Günther 6
Reinhardt, Fw., Hans-Günther 186
Rice, Lt., Robert 251
Richde, Fhr., 284
Richter, Lt., Erhard 54, 56
Riehl, Uffz., 265, 296
Riemer, Uffz., Toni 268, 292
Ritter, Uffz. 140
Roberts, Major 160
Roden, Fw., Erwin 56, 93, 123, 158
Rohwer, Oblt., Detlev 40, 53, 54, 104
Rolin, Sgt., Denys 18
Rombaut, Uffz., Guido 185, 186
Römer, Hptm., Harald 213
Roosevelt, President, Franklin D. 102
Rosenbroom, Lt, Hans-Folkert 10, 20
Rost, Uffz., Günther 148
Roth, mechanic 65,

Rudel, Obst., Hans-Ulrich 286
Rudschinat, Uffz., Siegfried 84, 118
Ruttau, Uffz., Walter 196
Saller, Fw., Martin 210
Sanden, Oblt. 199
Sannemann, Lt., Heinrich 9, 17
Sauer, Fw. 194
Scharler, Uffz., Franz 186
Scheu, Uffz., Erich 55
Schilling, Lt., Harald 210
Schlennstedt, Gefr., Werner 130
Schlichting, Oblt., Joachim 9, 10, 19, 22
Schmaul, Ogfr. 74
Schmid, Uffz., Otto 58, 77, 86, 120
Schmidt, Ofhr., 53
Schmitt, Lt., Rudolf 293
Schmude, Oblt., Hortari 25, 115
Schnappauf, Uffz., Rudolf 163, 170, 267
Schnoor, Hptm., Emil-Rudolf 105, 117, 118, 123, 125, 126, 159, 160, 163, 179, 193, 194, 200, 207, 210-12, 225, 229-31
Scholz, Hptm., Günther 41
Schönrock, Uffz.123, 182, 186
Schott, Lt., Georg 127, 149, 160, 163, 170, 179, 181, 184, 188
Schramm, Uffz., Werner 54, 86
Schubert, Uffz., Hans 26
Schuhmacher, Ofw., Leo 113, 193, 199, 209, 227-29, 234, 236, 255
Schulz, Hptm.186
Schulz, Uffz., Ernst 15
Schumacher, Obstlt., Carl 6, 7, 8, 41
Schwabedissen, General 85
Schwarz, Lt., Heinz 183
Seeliger, Hptm., Heinrich 6
Seeling, Fw., 292
Segatz, Oblt., Hermann 41, 207, 216, 225, 227
Selbach, Oberzahlm., Hans 130, 168
Selle von, Major, Erich 41, 55
Siegfried, Hptm., Ludwig 230, 246, 248, 251, 264, 296
Sill, Uffz., Günthor 283
Snaidero, Fw., Franz 79, 80, 81, 84
Sommer, Lt., 246
Sommer, Oblt., Gerhard 105, 116
Specht, Hptm., Günther 105, 127, 140
Spreckels, Uffz., Robert 118
Staerk, Oblt.163, 186, 199
Stahn, Uffz, Fritz 20
Staiger, Hptm., Hermann 264, 265, 280, 285
Stanowky, Sgt., Josef 282
Steeb, Fw., Erwin 286
Steffen, Lt. 194
Steiger, Lt., 37
Steiner, Uffz., Franz 118
Steinhoff, Lt., Johannes 6, 8
Stellfeld, Uffz., Robert 56, 92, 123
Stenschke, Ofhr., 292
Stiegler, Uffz., Helmut 227, 228, 236
Stiemer, Ofhr., 265, 268, 293
Stöcker, Uffz., 292
Stoffel, Lt., Siegfried 250-52
Stolte, Oblt., Paul 24, 27, 28, 31, 55
Stöwer, Uffz., Heinz 60, 86
Strauss, Fw., 292
Strich, Hptm., Friedrich 285
Strickrock, Gefr., Amandus 285
Strohal, Oblt., Rolf 56, 136, 137, 160, 179, 186, 194, 195
Strössner, Oblt., Rolf 41, 46, 49
Strunz, Uffz., Georg 102
Strutzina, Gefr. 74, 130
Sundermeier, Lt., Karl-Heinz 264
Swoboda, Uffz., Hubert 158, 160, 198, 199, 210, 227, 229, 230, 236, 238, 249, 264, 266, 286

Szlenkier, Tadeusz 282
Taube, Uffz., Paul 255
Tautz, Uffz., 291
Terborg, Lt., Ernst 58, 68, 91
Thieme, Uffz., Alfred 159
Thies, Ofw., 217
Timm, Fw., Fritz 56, 104, 106, 128, 181, 236, 238
Tismer, Uffz., Arthur 20
Tratt, Hptm., Eduard 144, 154
Trautloft, Oberst, Hannes 186
Triebel, Ofgr., Werner 233
Tröger, Lt., Heinz 87, 125, 148, 149
Tschira, Lt., Wilhelm 88, 124, 132, 149
Ubben, Maj., Kurt 234
Ücke, Gefr. 130, 167, 184
Ullman, Lt., Freimut 134, 150, 158
Vermaaten, Oblt., Hans 264
Vogel, Uffz., Rudolf 20, 254
Volleman, Louis 280
Völz, Uffz. Hermann 286
Vorhauer, Uffz., Hans 102, 160
Wachsmuth, Uffz. 25
Wagner, Uffz., Ullrich 262
Wainwright, Lt., Roger H. 252
Wasserzier, Lt., Herbert 21, 23
Watson, Lt., Lawrence 252
Weber, Hptm., Karl-Heinz 238, 247
Wedel, Fw., Ernst 297
Wedding, Oblt., Wolff-Kraft 24, 32, 36, 37
Wegner, Oblt., Fritz 158, 166, 174, 187, 190, 209, 246, 248, 249, 251, 264, 280, 282, 285, 286
Weninger, Uffz., Karl 160
Wennekers, Uffz., Hans-Gerd 33, 36, 37, 43, 46, 52, 56, 105, 115, 116, 128
Wickop, Hptm., Dietrich 54, 82, 103, 105, 123, 124, 125, 126, 132, 140, 141, 148
Wiegmann, Lt., Friedrich 125
Wieser, Lt., Josef 160
Windbichler, Lt., Hans 160
Winkler, Uffz., Ernst 48, 53, 54, 67, 103, 123, 26
Wintergerst, Lt., Eugen 124, 134, 149, 152, 154, 160, 175, 179, 181, 184
Witt, Oblt., Günther 108
Witzmann, Oblt., Edgar 227
Wloschinski, Uffz., Eugen 56, 113, 158, 159
Woitke, Hptm., Erich 250, 254, 255, 261, 264, 266
Woldenga, Major, Bernhard 9, 10, 11, 15
Wolf, Uffz., Albin37, 39, 43, 51, 95
Wollenweber, Oblt., 292, 296, 297
Worm, Gefr., Anton 103
Xiezopolski, F/O 105
Zander, Ofw. Friedrich 261, 267
Zemke, Col. "Hub" 226
Zick, Uffz., Siegfried 25, 35, 37, 39, 43, 51, 96
Zipprecht, Oblt. 296
Zober, Maj. Werner 294, 296
Zulauf, Ofhr., Erich 216
Zuzic, Oblt., Herwig 124, 140, 159, 161, 166, 178, 179, 181, 182, 183, 184